FAMILY STORIES, POETRY AND WOMEN'S W

Social Fictions Series

Series Editor
Patricia Leavy
USA

The *Social Fictions* series emerges out of the arts-based research movement. The series includes full-length fiction books that are informed by social research but written in a literary/artistic form (novels, plays, and short story collections). Believing there is much to learn through fiction, the series only includes works written entirely in the literary medium adapted. Each book includes an academic introduction that explains the research and teaching that informs the book as well as how the book can be used in college courses. The books are underscored with social science or other scholarly perspectives and intended to be relevant to the lives of college students—to tap into important issues in the unique ways that artistic or literary forms can.

Please email queries to pleavy7@aol.com

International Editorial Advisory Board

Carl Bagley, University of Durham, UK
Anna Banks, University of Idaho, USA
Carolyn Ellis, University of South Florida, USA
Rita Irwin, University of British Columbia, Canada
J. Gary Knowles, University of Toronto, Canada
Laurel Richardson, The Ohio State University (Emeritus), USA

Family Stories, Poetry and Women's Work

Knit Four, Frog One (Poems)

By

Sandra L. Faulkner
Bowling Green State University, USA

SENSE PUBLISHERS
ROTTERDAM / BOSTON / TAIPEI

A C.I.P. record for this book is available from the Library of Congress.

ISBN 978-94-6209-846-6 (paperback)
ISBN 978-94-6209-847-3 (hardback)
ISBN 978-94-6209-848-0 (e-book)

Published by: Sense Publishers,
P.O. Box 21858, 3001 AW Rotterdam, The Netherlands
https://www.sensepublishers.com/

Printed on acid-free paper

"Faulkner's *Family Stories, Poetry and Women's Work: Knit Four, Frog One* takes readers into the personal lives of four generations of mothers and daughters, poetically uncovering concrete aspects of social processes of family, motherhood, relationships, and writing. A fusion of social science and art that invites engagement of all your senses to understand the felt truth of lived experience." – Carolyn Ellis, Distinguished University Professor, Department of Communication, University of South Florida

"Captivating, nuanced, and often surprising, Faulkner's work is a vital contribution that bridges the chasm between traditional interpersonal communication research and brave new artistic worlds for relationship studies. Readers will find that *Knit Four/Frog One* offers as much for the heart as it does for the mind: a poetic, candid, and highly personal glimpse into feminism and family. I cannot wait to share this book with others!" – Jimmie Manning, Ph.D., Associate Professor of Communication, Undergraduate Program Director, Department of Communication, Affiliate Women, Gender, & Sexuality Studies Program, Northern Illinois University

"Through this book, Faulkner presents a refreshing way of understanding, researching, and teaching about the communication in families. Scholars, practitioners, and students will find critical insight into important issues including women's roles, privacy management, stigmatized identities, and the influence of social structure on personal relationships in this volume. The discussion questions and exercises make this book an excellent tool for teaching interpersonal communication, family communication, and women's studies in an innovative way." – Pamela J. Lannutti, Associate Professor and Director, Graduate Program in Professional and Business Communication, Department of Communication, La Salle University

"Born from Faulkner's own ambivalence about her pregnancy and personal difficulties transitioning to the role of mother, *Family Stories, Poetry, and Women's Work/Knit Four, Frog One (Poems)* re-imagines the meaning(s) of motherhood in the context of family storytelling. Sandra's innovative arts-based social science text demystifies poetic inquiry, providing readers both an embodied example of excellence and detailed exercises for use when practicing one's own craft." – Elizabeth A. Suter, PhD, Associate Professor, Director of Undergraduate Studies, Department of Communication Studies, University of Denver

In *Knit Four, Frog One,* Sandra L. Faulkner knits her life as mother, daughter and granddaughter; as wife, runner and lover into a rainbow-hued shawl of lived experience the reader can wrap around herself—balm and body armor, both. By turns fierce and funny, coolly observant and tenderly vulnerable, these poems show Faulkner's great range of subject matter and form. From transcriptions of dinner time conversations with intractable four-year-olds, to instruction manuals about how to survive an infant; through sonnets written to a husband's newly diagnosed cancer, and visual collages that bring together family ephemera and photos, the landscape of the book is nubby and various and truly tactile. This is a writer who knows how to wield her tools—memory, pen and needle —and with them creates a worthy portrait of a family who paint their "church-house doors harlot red on Easter weekend," who resist, smartly and beautifully, "the messy art of containment." – Sheila Squillante, author of *In This Dream of My Father* and *Women Who Pawn Their Jewelry,* Editor-in-chief of *The Fourth River Literary Journal,* Associate editor of *PANK Magazine,* Associate Director MFA Program in Creative Writing and Assistant Professor of English at Chatham University

For all of the Miriams, great and small.

TABLE OF CONTENTS

PREFACE

This book is a memoir in poetry about family stories, mother-daughter relationships, women's work, mothering, writing, family secrets, and patterns of communication in close relationships. It can be read for pleasure as a collection of poetry or used as a springboard for reflection and discussion in courses such as family communication, sociology of gender and the family, psychology of women, relational communication, and women's studies. Family stories anchor family culture and provide insight into relational and family life. They also create family; communication takes place inside families and offers us a way to sustain, create and alter family culture. In addition to a collection of family stories, this work may be used as a teaching tool to get you to think about the stories that we tell and don't tell in families and the importance of how family is created and maintained in our stories. I believe that the use of poetry to tell family stories reveals the emotions and the rhythms of family life and narration in ways that prose alone cannot. Poetry lets me goodwill my secure cloak of citations, argue in verse that there is space for critical work and personal experience in the study of close relationships (Faulkner, 2012a). I begin this introduction by telling you how I came to write "social science poems" and how you can use them in your own writing, reflection, and understanding of family stories.

I came to the poetry project I present here because I needed a way to write about my grandmother and mother when I gave birth to my own daughter in 2009. I resisted and (re)played their questions and advice about relationships in my stubborn head as I struggled with my ambivalence about pregnancy and the mother role (Faulkner, 2012b). I wrote an essay about the first year of my daughter's life and my difficult and anxious adjustment to role of mother (Faulkner, 2014), but I need to add a poetic rendering of what mother means to me in the context of family and my relationships to women. The social scientist turned to poetry as I had done during other stressful times in my life. This collection of poems represents my marriage of social science and art, the culmination of thirteen years of poetic inquiry, using poetry as/in/for research (Faulkner,

2009). I wrote (bad) poems during my adolescence and even corresponded with an English teacher for a summer in middle school about my poetry. I picked up poetry (again) when I was doing post-doctoral work at Penn State and continued with community-writing workshops in Syracuse, NY when I worked as an interpersonal communication scholar in a tenure track position. Writing poetry helped me recover from my training in graduate school and the numbing realities of academic writing. It helped me reclaim creativity and its rhythms.

I write poetry because I am a "bad" social scientist. I believe in poetic truths more than social science Truth punctuated with a capital T. I study and teach about personal relationships, but I'm most interested in relationship-ing, what relationships feel like and sound like and smell like more than how they function as an analytic variable. I imagine poetry ripples like the waves of an MRI scan to mirror the stories of our relationships. Poetry can be the waves. Poetry can help us see a relationship bleeding out, hemorrhaging from the inside, spilling outside the neat axioms of theory in a puddle of messy fluids. Poetry can have us experience the social structures and ruptures in situ as we read, as we listen, as we hold our breath waiting for the next line. Poetry is salve.

In the poetry collection titled *Knit Four, Frog One*, I knit connections between a DIY (do-it-yourself) value, economics, and family culture through the use of confessional poetry (i.e. poetry of the personal/I). The poems and images trouble four generations of women in my family and "women's work" of mothering, cooking and crafting. I write the story of Miriam (my maternal grandmother), Barbara (my mother), Sandra (me), and Miriam May aka Mimi (my daughter) in what I call "a memoir in verse." The poetry voices the themes of economic and collective family self-reliance and speaks to cultural discourses of feminist resistance and resilience, relational and personal identities. The memoir plays with the tensions of aesthetic value and epistemic worth through the use of personal and academic voices (Gingrich-Philbrook, 2005).

I wrote these poems and present them in an academic forum *as poetry* to show what poetic inquiry can do. I wrote this book to record stories for my daughter, as a love letter to the women in my life, and an explanation for why my daughter is named Miriam for my mother's mom, my grandmother, Miriam, the first and great. I wrote this book as arts-based social science.

I write poetry because I miss my nineteen year-old self, and in particular, the self without formal social science training. She sees things that Doctor Faulkner cannot see, and she comes out to play in my poetry. I like Faulkner's poetic persona, how writing poetry provides an escape for her into my everyday world. I like that poetry is a conversation between my personas, a recognition of how identities are multiple, fluid and sometimes contentious. I remember to pay attention to the pauses, to laugh when there are no words. Poetry becomes my way to voice the ineffable and reminds me when it is okay to let my passive aggressive side out to roar.

Family Stories as Women's Work

I learned to knit from a Stich 'n Bitch Handbook (Stoller, 2003), what I consider to be a kind of hipster guide to knitting, in the car on the way to my spouse's family farm. I never learned from my mother or grandmother, both of whom tried to teach me on more than one occasion. I am unable to pinpoint what my resistance to their lessons stemmed from, but I suspect that my young adult self found it too feminine and too domestic, too much like women's work. Besides, Nanny (my mom) and Grammy (my grandmother) gifted me hand knit and sewn items that were too beautiful to reproduce. I gave into knitting after Grammy died in May 2007. Stitching is a way to feel closer to her, to remember her in a way that she would have approved of because when I visited her near Philadelphia during my time as a graduate student at Penn State, we crafted together. And we talked about relationships as I present in the poem "1975 Singer *Athena 2000* Electronic Sewing Machine." She worried that my anti-marriage and anti-children zeal would portend a life as an old lonely woman.

The poetry in this collection theorizes how family stories serve multiple functions from protective to stifling. What stories get told, by whom, and to what effect is a form of creating the rules; what we need to coordinate behavior, guide action, tell us what is obligatory, what it means to be a member of the family, what is prohibited, and what is appropriate or irrelevant (Stone, 2003). Women are the ones who often promulgate and preserve family love, stories and rituals (Stone, 2003). Stories connect and promote a sense of family responsibility, even when family members have nothing in common. When read together, the poems present stories of confirmation and disconfirmation, humor as resilience and distraction, mothering as friendship and resistance to authority, craft as love, and love as useful work. Family themes are recurring attitudes, beliefs, and outlooks on life that can be seen by examining rules and looking at stories (Wilmot, 2003; Galvin, Brommel, & Bylund, 2004). My use of concrete poems (i.e., shape poetry that conveys the meaning of the poem through the typographical cues), which depict knitting stitches as section breaks focuses attention on the larger themes of *family origins* (knit stich), *becoming mother* (purl stitch), *relational difficulties* (hurdle stitch), and *crafting coherent narratives* (Kitchener stitch).

I liken the poetry here to a series of family stories, a memoir in poetry, if you will, a confessional tale for the ethnographers (Lindlof & Taylor, 2011), a (re)working of what is often women's work, the crafting of family narratives. I label the poetry here confessional because it is autobiographical and hope that it addresses and plays with the critique of confessional poetry as narcissistic, trivial, and sensational to "embrace a larger social vision, achieving revelation over narcissism, universal resonance over self-referential anecdote" (Graham & Sontag, p. 6). The poems are intended to focus attention on these issues rather than resolve them to show how the use of personal family intimacies (or the *impression* of the use of personal family intimacies) may be a way of constructing empowering family narratives. Another goal with this project is to use confessional poetry to interrogate and alter attitudes and create social change through the visibility of stigmatized identities (e.g., family definitions, feminist mother, ambivalent mother, feminist bisexual).

The stories and metaphors we use to describe family may just protect them (Pipher, 1997). The things told over and over again reveal what families want to believe about themselves, and the telling can help reconstruct families, especially when dangerous secrets are revealed and reworked for healing (Poulus, 2008). We see the adventure stories like in the poem "Mother/Daughter" wherein I show how my daughter craves action and being in charge just like her mother. We tell the award stories such as "SUBJECT: Becoming Midwestern Beige, PhD" with the narrator navigating the in-between world of the academy and home. The good deed stories are also important such as the care for others lauded in the poem, "Baby Ripple Blanket." And there is, of course, the cautionary tale outlined in "How to Date Catholic Boys."

Some of the poems in this collection use *accidental ethnography* as a technique to write about family, what Chris Poulus (2008) suggested as a method to story our lives and bring forward what may be lost in our unconscious—eating disorders, stigmatized identities, sexuality, abuse, and other difficult topics. This entails writing about dreams, clues, memories, and reflections from the unconscious, from seemingly "accidental signs and impulses that surge up and, from time to time, really grip us, take hold of us, call us out and throw us down, sweep us away, and carry us to places we may not have even imagined" (Poulus, 2008, p. 47). The goal of this kind of writing is to reveal and make conscious secrets that harm families and communities.

Accidental ethnography means writing and rewriting family secrets that haunt us and break into our day-to-day relating. If we write about hurtful secrets and reveal harmful patterns of interaction, then we may be able to tell better stories and offer more possibilities. For example, the found collage poem, "In the Court of Common Pleas," represents discovery and silence. My mother gave me a box of family papers and photos, in which I found the court papers for a custody case. My mother's maternal grandmother pleaded for custody of her daughters, but she lost the case because of accusations of adultery. I discovered (and reconstructed) a different and more nuanced tale than what my mother or grandmother had ever told me. I remember Grammy talking about her mother, Theresa, fondly (and not calling her *mother* may have been telling, too). The untold and court documented reason Miriam ended up living with her stepmother, Emily, and father was because of Theresa's alleged adultery making her unfit to mother in the court's eyes; I had always been told it was because of the divorce and her financial situation. My mother whispered the story of a childless police officer and his wife wanting to adopt my grandmother after her father, Harold, died, but Emily got custody of Miriam and her sister, Ruth. Emily had two daughters with Harold, so Miriam lived with Ruth and her half-sisters (Helen and Betty) in what I consider a house-full of strong women. When I asked my Aunt about the court case recently, she told me that Harold had been sleeping with Emily before he married her, and further, he only married her because she was pregnant. Thus, Harold shouldn't be considered as some wronged man, "He was just as guilty as Theresa." The family themes seep through the inked stories.

Family stories are one of the cornerstones of family culture and can provide insight into relational and family life. Think about the stories that get told and the ones that are not told in families and you will understand the importance of how family is storied and what we consider to constitute family. Much of what you learn about family and family relations is implicit and mute, thus poetry makes a good vehicle for crafting a dialectic of silence versus voice because as the poet, Dean Young (2010) asserts, poetry's strength is the ability to position dialectics. "A poem asserts itself as poetry by being in dialogue with what it resists" (p. 38). Young (2010) asked,

> How do we understand each other when we say I love you? To simplify, this is a distinction between a communicative state and an expressive state ... Poetry is in perpetual negotiation between these two urges. Between interior and exterior, between liberty and obligation, anarchy and order, self and community, referent and what it can refer to, sign and thing. (p. 39)

In the Appendix, I provide exercises designed to get you writing about family culture using poetry. Communication privacy management theory (Petronio, 2002) suggests that the revelation or concealment of family secrets depends on our motivation for disclosing, as well as what family disclosure rules are in place. For example, you may notice that some of the poems discuss sexuality, though a general family rule when I was growing up meant silence about personal family business to outsiders. The difference between personal motivation and the need to disclose family secrets that violate family disclosure rules creates turbulence. However, topic avoidance can lead to dissatisfaction.

The ethical implications of revealing and deciding to conceal secrets may be addressed if we talk through definitions of family and the function family serves in our lives. It may be obvious that there is no ideal family, that in fact, families are social constructions (Wood, 2002). The definition of family can refer to families of procreation and origin, including nuclear and extended family residing in one household, who have established biological or socio-legal legitimacy because of shared genetics, marriage or adoption. We can also consider family to be interdependent individuals who work to fulfill psychosocial tasks that help with mutual need fulfilment, nurturance and development. Family can be a network of people who live together over long periods of time bound by ties of marriage, blood, or commitment, legal *or* otherwise (Galvin et al., 2004). After Grammy's father died when she was nine, her stepmother, Emily, and her stepmother's friend, "Auntie Lou," stepped in to raise her and her sisters. When I was growing up, family friends were often called Aunt and Uncle. My spouse and I also refer to close friends as Aunt and Uncle and celebrate family milestones together at "family dinners." These are all examples of an expanded definition of family and the idea that there can be families of choice (Wood, 2002). We create family in communication; communication takes place inside families, creates and sustains them. Family is transactional and more than a string of dyads; family represents a group and can be studied from a group perspective (Beck, Miller & Frahm, 2012). Thus, it may be best to consider family as a group of intimates who generate a sense of home and group identity, experience strong ties of loyalty and emotion, and share a sense of history and a future (Wood, 2002).

Once you understand family patterns represented in stories, then you can see if you repeat any of them and can understand how family helps resist or adapt to outside forces and crises that arise (Koerner & Fitzpatrick, 2008). Thus, the storying of relational (and family) life is important. Discourse within families may be especially important in non-traditional families (Galvin, 2006). Relationships are enacted and formed through the relational members' communication processes and, in turn, the nature of the relationship is influenced by ongoing communication between the members. Relational messages influence our self-concepts; talking to others in our families about our feelings for them can increase or decrease self-worth (Dailey, 2010). We can enact affection through the use of *confirming messages* that make one value the self more, directly acknowledge the other, offer supportive and positive feedback, and clarifying responses better than *disconfirming messages* that make one devalue the self (Dailey, 2006).

POETIC INQUIRY AS INTERPERSONAL COMMUNICATION RESEARCH

> The poetic representations of lives is never just an end in itself. The goal is political, to change the way we think about people and their lives and to use the poetic-performative format to do this. The poet makes the world visible in new and different ways, in ways ordinary social science writing does not allow. The poet is accessible, visible, and present in the text, in ways that traditional writing forms discourage. (Denzin, 2014, p. 86)

The poems I offer you here can be considered a poetic inquiry into family stories. Poetry can be used as a tool and method for presentation of research data, as a source of data, and as a source for data analysis (Faulkner, 2009). In a meta-analysis of 234 poetic inquiry sources, Prendergast (2009) uncovered three kinds of voices present in poetry used as social science research, that of the researcher, the participants, and the literature. She argued that the majority of the work used researcher-voiced poems, which emphasized the experience of the poet-researcher using field notes, journals, and reflective writing as data for the poems. This is the kind of poetry you find in *Knit Four, Frog One*. I constructed these poems from family documents, my memories, conversational interviews with my mother and aunt, and events I witnessed and/or heard about from family members. The poems represent family stories voiced from my perspective, though the poet and essayist, Mark Doty (2010) reminds us that perception is always limited; "All accounts, it seems, are partial; thus all perception might be said to be tentative, an opportunity for interpretation, a guessing game" (p. 5). I wish to emphasize the idea of perception to demonstrate my concern with relational ethics (Ellis, 2007). I sent my mother the collage poems for Mother's Day, and I admit to being nervous about her reaction. They were already published in an on-line literary magazine. She called me to say that she liked them and that she may, in fact, be the only person who would understand them and find them meaningful. I am not sure how she will react when she sees the rest of the poems together in this collection, but again, this is my telling, and the details and scenes I selected to represent are the ones wherein I am a central character.

As you read the collection, you may notice it is not always entirely clear whose voice you hear. This is intentional to show how stories become part of a larger conversation when they are spoken and to show the limitations of perception. The ambiguity also speaks to the way that memory works and the difficulty of describing our experiences.

> We cannot rely on words to convey to another person what it is like to be ourselves … But we have nothing else, and when words are tuned to their highest ability, deployed with the strengths the most accomplished poets bring to bear on the project of saying what's here before us—well, it is possible to feel, at least for a moment, language clicking into place, into a relation with the world that feels seamless and inevitable. If this is a dream so be it. (Doty, 2010, p. 10)

Poetic Inquiry Goals

I use poetry as/in/for social science research, in particular interpersonal communication research about families, to accomplish three goals: (1) to marry social science and poetry; (2) to effect social change through a focus on the aesthetic; and (3) to use poetry as a pedagogical tool for the study of relational communication.

Social Science + Poetry. First, I wrote these poems to connect the personal with my work life, the creative work with my social science training. I use dialogue poems as a way to incorporate dialectics into this collection and to give voice to the both/and. When I had an infant and no maternity leave, it became a necessity to adopt dialogical thinking and refute the false binary between private and public conceptions of relationships (Baxter, 2011). I did not have time to think of the social scientist and the poet as mutually exclusive roles. My life situation required the ability to do work in my head while I nursed my child, struggled to stay awake between classes, and generally not lose my (work) mind. All of my work had to fit into smaller pockets of time. I discovered that poetry writing fits into small spaces, and that social science theorizing can be poetry, especially if we consider that "the ethnographer's writing self **cannot not** be present, there is **no** objective space outside the text" (Denzin, 2014, p. 26).

Through poetic analysis, a technique of using poems as data for qualitative research, I make an explicit connection between poetry and interpersonal relationships by detailing what it means to be a woman in my family and the demonstration of crafting relationships as vital women's work. This analysis and subsequent representation serve as an exemplar of how poetry offers interpersonal communication practitioners an explicit demonstration of individual's needs to poeticize their everyday relational challenges (Pelias, 2011). This critical writing helped me articulate personal experiences and connect to larger culture structures to explain the meaning of mothering for a white, middle-class, highly educated, snarky feminist woman (cf. Faulkner, 2014).

The communication scholars, Leslie Baxter and Dawn Braithwaite (2008), contend that interpersonal research and theory is biased toward post-positivist methods. Their content analysis of published studies in two popular relational journals from 1990-2005 showed that 83.3% took a post-positivist stance, with 13.9% adopting an interpretive stance and 2.9% a critical perspective. This suggests to me that there exists room for poetry as/in/for relational research. Prendergast (2009) argued that the best poetic inquiry is that which concerns itself with affect as well as intellect and deals with topics grounded in the "affective experiential domain." The use of family stories as a basis for autoethnographic poetry represents human thought in an affective context (McAdams, 1993). The impulse to create poetry is like the impulse toward narrative, and narratives provide, at least in part, a window into our thoughts, behavior, and experiences. Narratives allow a way to examine identities, the communicative behavior that externalizes our thoughts about identity (Faulkner & Hecht, 2011), how we make sense of our cultural and social worlds, and how we try and create coherence (Lieblich, Tuval-Mashiach, & Zilber, 1998). In many instances, we narrate particular life experiences where there is a rift between a real and ideal self, between the self and society (Riessman, 1993).

Social Change. The use of creative social science was important to evoke the aesthetics of change and for the poetry to resonate with readers, for audiences to experience the poetry as "evocative mediators" of painful relational experiences and recognize and tell their own stories (Todres & Galvin, 2008, p. 571). Because poetry focuses on the minutiae of language use and form to not only present but also create an experience for the reader, it makes a valuable contribution to our understanding of personal relationships. Poetry matters because its powerful, the fact that it "serves up the substance of our lives, and becomes more than a mere articulation of experience, although that articulation alone is part of its usefulness…it allows us to see ourselves freshly and keenly. It makes the invisible world visible" (Parini, 2008, p. 181). It can hep us shape lives in ways that we want to live; we create and tell the stories that we need. As Denzin (2014) reminds us "to argue for a factually correct picture of a 'real' person is to ignore how persons are created in performances" (p. 13). The poet's focus on form is important for meaning making in poetry.

> Form is the visible side of content. The way in which the content becomes manifest. Form: time turning into space and space turning into time simultaneously…We name one thing and then another. That's how time enters poetry. Space, on the other hand, comes into being through the attention we pay to each word. The more intense our attention, the more space, and there's a lot of space inside words. (Simic, 1990, p. 85)

Form and language are also intimately connected. Pelias (2011) eloquently stated that "Constituted in interaction, I am formed by the language that passes between me and others. And I make sense of my relationships by finding a language that provides some account of my personal observations and feelings" (p. 17). The language of poetry demonstrates how communication is relational, how we create identities, and how we feel our way through our relationships.

The use of poetry to examine family relationships can be categorized as performative writing because the personal experiences of the researcher are connected to the ethnographic project (Denzin, 2014), the writing takes shape through observation and field experience to bring the audience the most interesting and complex moments of our lived experience (Pelias 2005). "Language and speech do not mirror experience; rather, they create representations of experience. Meanings are always in motion, inclusive conflicting, contradictory. There are gaps between reality, experience, and performances" (Denzin, 2014, p. 37). Using writing that is both performative and poetic allows me to represent family stories in a "messy" format that speaks to representational issues of empowerment and disempowerment (Alcoff, 2003). Poetry as an experience can create empathy in an audience by allowing them to see and feel what the writer does (Pelias, 2005).

The radical subjectivity of my experiences can make larger claims of the importance of particularized experiences in larger structures of family. Using performative writing, specifically poetry, to examine family communication provides insight into underlying values of how to do relationships, and in this case, how communication plays a role before, during, and after they end (Pelias, 2011). The power of poetry to reconnect our selves to loss, conscious and unconscious hurts that manifest in our relational interactions, offers interpersonal scholars, educators, and those in relationships other ways of understanding. In another project, I interviewed poets about their conceptions of good and bad poetry. Phil Memmer told me that there is too much niceness in poetry and argued that good poetry challenges us; it has the potential to hurt feelings because "the stakes are high."

Can you write the poem that's going to make your mother weep? ... And not because you hate your mother, not your mom who you can't stand who would never let you do anything you want to do and you don't want to be around and haven't spoken to in ten years … But your mom who does everything for you [and] who you love talking to and adore, and you know these poems will upset her. Can you push hard enough on your work to do that because it's something you believe in and something you want to write, a story you think has to be told? And push hard enough to accomplish what you hope to accomplish with it, not let yourself off.

Family stories mean that we are telling what we need to tell, even if they make your mother cry. I imagine that not every member of my family, actually any member of my family, would tell this particular story, but I pay close attention to craft to make the story resonant inside and outside the family boundaries.

Ars Poetica. Finally, I use poetry as a pedagogical tool because this kind of writing, in my experience, speaks more to students than traditional social science writing. I often begin classes with poems that spark the day's lesson and decided to edit a collection of creative cases in relational communication for use when teaching about relationships (Faulkner, 2013). Thus, this book is meant to be a teaching tool in addition to a collection of family stories in verse. In the Appendix, I offer some discussion questions you may use when you read the poems. In the poetry here, you will notice a few *ars poetica* (e.g., Memo to Faulkner from the Fluff and Fold), poems about the art of poetry, that I include as a way to demonstrate my concern with craft, my ideas about poetry, and a way to read my poems (Faulkner, 2009). Alternatively, here is my latest *ars poetica* in prose:

> The language of poetry, when properly absorbed, becomes part of our private vocabulary, our way of moving through the world. Poetry matters, and without it we can live only partially, not fully conscious of the possibilities (emotional and intellectual) that life affords. (Parini, 2008, p. xiv)

Poetry, in particular, allows me to be a better social scientist. I want you to do more than think about your own live; I want you to critique how social structures scaffold your experiences of relating. Poetry embodies experience to show truths that are not usually evident, to seduce and empower readers. Our deeply ingrained ideas about gender and culture and class and race, the seemingly natural ways of being are easier to unravel in verse (e.g., Faulkner, Calafell, & Grimes, 2009). As the poet Jay Parini (2008) wrote, "As a language adequate to out experience, poetry allows us to articulate matters of concern in such a way that they become physical, tangible, and immediate" (p. 25). Poems allow me to show a range of meanings, which makes most sense to me as someone who is interested in people's stories and how these stories make meaning(full) lives.

I can say things in poetic lines that can't be stated in other ways.

I think poetry because it is a habit. I cannot take a run without working out lines on the exhales. The interpersonal axiom, you cannot not communicate, transformed into a habitual I cannot not write poetry. Standing in line, taking a shower, feeding my kid, waking up before anyone else in the house, waiting and more waiting are all contexts for poetry writing. I am living the ethnographic poet's life (Rose, 1990). The biggest challenge for me is to focus on the aesthetic dimensions of the writing, to merge the different selves that bring in empirical research, personal experience and observation with the need to expand my story to *our* story. "The pleasure of recognizing a described world is no small thing" (Doty, 2010, p. 11).

ACKNOWLEDGEMENTS

Gratitude to the editors of the following journals in which these poems first appeared: *Damselfly* (Remodeling Dream), *gravel* (my memories are mother; In the Court of Common Pleas), *Mom Egg Review* (How to potty train when presenting a paper on maternal poetry), *Sugar House Review* (Farm Trilogy), *Storm Cellar* (Pacifier Ode), *NorthWoods Journal* (Telemarketers; Leaving Paul for the Plane to the Sex Conference).

The following poems will (re)appear in my chapbook *Knit Four, Make One* from Kattywompus Press: "Farm Trilogy," "When the preacher came by the house after our year absence," "Make Two," "Letter to Faulkner from the Fluff and Fold" (renamed Memo to Faulkner from the Fluff and Fold), "Teachers" (renamed Mother/Daughter), "Pacifier Ode," "Instructions for Surviving Infant," "How to potty train when presenting a manuscript on maternal poetry," "Baby Ripple Blanket," "Bedtime Story," "Invitation to a Dead Grandmother," "HURDLE STITCH," "Hoagland writes to Faulkner about Thingitude," "Dead Leg Ode," "At the Viewing," "Suicide Window, Detroit" (renamed Suicide Window, Toledo), "Doing Dishes," "Remodeling Dream."

"Invitation to a Dead Grandmother" first appeared in *Small Batch: An Anthology of Bourbon Poems*, Leigh Anne Hornfeldt & Teneice Durrant, (Eds.), 2013, pp. 92-93. Lexington, KY: Two of Cups Press.

Parts of the preface were adapted from Faulkner, S. L. (2012). Frogging It: A poetic analysis of relationship dissolution. *Qualitative Research in Education, 1*(2), 202-227. Available at: http://www.hipatiapress.com/hpjournals/index.php/qre/article/view/373

Thanks to Patricia Leavy, one of my feminist heroines, for her enthusiastic support of this project and all things arts-based research.

ACKNOWLEDGEMENTS

My (former) poetry teacher (always) and friend, Sheila Squillante, served as quality assurance by helping me fine-tune the aesthetics and sequencing of the poems.

KNIT FOUR, FROG ONE

Poems

Mimi: Mommy, did you know that some books are true
      and some books are not true?
      Some books are make-believe.

MOTHER/GRAND/DAUGHTER

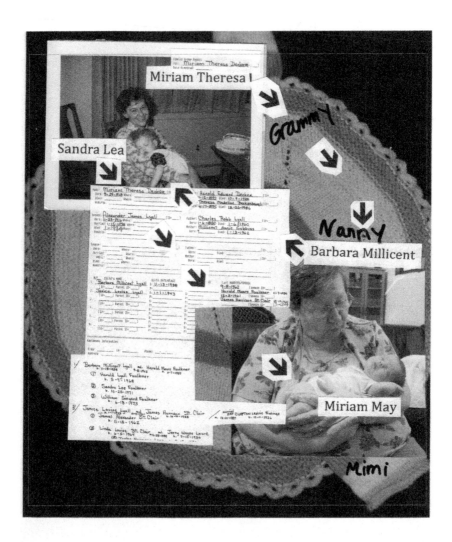

KNIT STITCH

through the loop

pull the loop

on the left needle

in back

with the yarn

Eating Dinner

Mom: If you do. not. stop. KICKING
the table, mom and dad are going to the store
and leaving you here with the dog.

Mimi: If mom and dad go to the store and leave me at home alone, I
will call the police, I will dial 911. They will come and put
you in jail. Then they will take me away, and I will live with
another family.

Mom: And would you be sad?

Mimi: No.

Farm Trilogy

I. Throwing Sticks at Cows

The boulder crouched
between the pasture trees,
mostly Georgia pines,
as if waiting for us
to bring the smell of summer,
peanut butter or mayonnaise
on white bread wiped with sweat.
The trail through the woods
was scratched on our knees,
barbed wire torn shorts,
the fun of kid made cammo,
shimming around granite,
hiding from old Vaughter's
shotgun and scowl.
Do you remember
when you were still Billy
and those trees green
above smelly ripe piles,
our bouquets of honeysuckle
for mom, pockets filled
with roly poly and pine straw
before the suburb bought
the Farm cheap, marked it
with a historic metal plaque?
I can't make myself see
if the boulder is still there
hidden from the groomed trail
paved with traffic, waiting
for us to leg-up with naked elbows
and our impromptu sandwiches.

II. Driving Miss Mimi

We drive south from the strange
wet prairies, the Great Black Swamp
drained for farms, ditches filled
with grey pebbles and icy trash,
young-green winter wheat sprouts
before the wail of the tractor pulls,

from this unexpected open
width of sky, dirt and fear of wet
encasements, mosquitos and inundations
where I moved for the love of naming letters
birthed a girl and books despite
a professed milk sickness.

We drive down 75 toward my familiar
Georgia pines, long needles that smell
like Girl Scout camp, damp polyester shorts.
The pound puppy in the front seat
snores, shifts and sniffs
as his usual scents turn strange.

Stone Mountain lichens cling to granite:
My infant's head slithers down
the restraint, spit glues paci to her chin
suspended like an extra seat-belt.
This first trip we stop too often,
to feed, change and express

exhaustion, my over-active let-down means
breast feeding is like shot-gunning
beer—ball point pen jabs a hole
in cold aluminum—gulps
of bubbles and sweet liquid
in the back seat. My spouse knows

my soliloquies about public lactating:
convenience store magazines splashed
with bared breasts, X. Conspersa
exposed in pools of fluorescent light
compete with my mossy mother rant:
"I should feed her by the chips, candy
bars and condoms." The sneaky places

we stole away from band practice,
skipped school for the art gallery
to buy laffy taffy, Tab, and rolos.
Kids too tame to walk bad:
my familiar South.

III. Running with Buddy on KK Highway, Rogersville, MO

Rexall drug pregnancy test crushed in the ditch,
directions peed on, Keystone and Bud Light
boxes, cans smashed, plastic tubes sunk
in mud from a deserted meth lab, this college bitch
runs the ditch along the dairy farm
that grew my spouse, where trash collects

this college teacher runs here
where trash collects because they work
with hands in the dirt, while I work
on my morning coffee, watch uncle Ed
get the gun and then the skunk
bent and already half gone

from some farm accident, already half gone,
some accident on the farm, this cautious
family planner only popped out one,
no accidents, no car accordioned in the ditch—
why the dog is on a leash—
my kid asks about all that poop

the collateral damage on her boots,
the high maintenance dog whines like a prince
as tractors and 4-wheelers whine
to keep the farm through drought
but it is not enough, the cows went, gone
since Tuesday, loaded and lifted into trucks

no more black and white dots canvassing the hills

When the preacher came by the house after our year absence

the adults stood
rooted by the gardenias
too busy with the visit
to scold us
for big wheels upended
spokes bent and dead,
in the yard for the sandman,
forgotten, we pretend to play
to catch some words
they pretend we don't hear
this Sunday after church
where we only attend
our driveway worship.
My dad's voice as never:
Why so long—
did you not notice?
your Christianity means no
Black children at church—
Preacher's voice rises in prayer:
—misunderstood, not so
long, no, not prejudiced—
They pretend we don't hear,
no invitation inside
no coffee or mom's fudge,
all the little children
not welcome in this world.

SUBJECT: Becoming Midwestern Beige, PhD

Dear Colleagues, Here's to all things Midwest
to canning and knitting to passive aggressive niceness
(e.g., see memo below) to bringing you cold tea,
a stack of plastic glasses and a pitcher of ice
to quench the pain of moving here
to tractor pulls and fried bologna,
to only pretending to be a local if it helps
and to really changing your license plates and address
so the court knows where to call.
I find the flat green view of plants and more plants
as particular as our neighbor's love letters
sent via the City on official letterhead
with suggestions for how to maintain the lawn
which must not creep onto the sidewalk,
all overhung like the degrees on my wall.
So sorry you cannot decipher the police officer's calling card
tucked far inside the mailbox with a plea
about your dog serenading the backyard sun,
which I must note shines in such proximity to Indiana
that Northwest Ohio may indeed be the Midwest
despite your erudite objections
(cite: census bureau data confirms).

I hereby present my Midwest Curriculum Vitae
my tenured contributions:

2013 Canning total: 22 quarts of tomatoes; 12 pints of pickles;
7 pints of corn salsa; 10-1/2 pints mild salsa and 6 pints of peach
salsa; 3 quarts of slow-roasted tomato spaghetti sauce.

Validity Data: burned knuckles and collapsed arches,
one white, blue-eyed girl conceived on Black Swamp soil
while cutting and pasting together a winning portfolio.

Awards: Blue ribbon for knitted poncho @Wood County Fair
(Most of which I knit in your meetings
like your mom knit at practices and appointments,
purling a fence to keep out the pretend dialogue-
before my needles were confiscated at the grand jury.
I am expert enough to consider a jab with a needle,
a gash big enough to require some stitches.)

This is our Midwest where you can spit
across the landscape for states and states
with these misdemeanors, commit felonies in your mind,
deny data with the research you word and spin.

Make Two

With two needles and a ball of string,
we learn the art of multiplication—

2 couplets, lovers, dyads, pet rats,
not twins like in my preggo horror movie.

Two tickets to a concert, a table for 2.
Not my favorite number-the rent is past due.

II, 2, two ways to write the number, my favorite
curvy because you can lie

in the bottom, the bowl. The number of bites
you need to share, a joint account. Two.

The usual number of cake layers, the pieces
of toast you get with eggs, the # of eggs

in the daily special, my good and bad side,
dichotomy, either   or (not both/and),

one part of a compound sentence. Two sides
to the bed, two dimensions, two favorite colors,

the number of legs Dad once had,
knit in front and back=M1, 2 stitches,

what you need to erase a day, not the number
after birth, 2 parts water, 2 ounces of bourbon.

On My 30th Birthday, I Leave Paul for the Plane to the Sex
Conference

I tell myself to breathe, but his celery-scented kiss won't dim;
shuffled conference papers, a raisin bagel, and piped in mandolin
force me to think about the awkward bore,
the crusty worries of dishes and birthdays that steal our sex will.
I consider this as I fly south to the sexy
conference where I will talk about sex without getting down.

I ask why this raging feminist feels knocked down
(like the cliché in my last poem), eyes dim
when he walks away to straddle his bike, all sexed-up
for mindful pedestrians like Madeline,
our neighbour with the bumper sticker—Wild-Women-Will.
She probably gets laid by a truckload of boars.

I tell him my work is a bore,
that talk about sex is not like eider down
you snuggle into at will,
it can't make me a Happy Hooker or dim
my thoughts about degrees of freedom or Mandy,
the super sexologist from Kinsey who's research is even sexy.

Paul leans in to tell me I'm sexy,
but I remind him of the truth, how boring
our daily details get, the man
who controls his child-support will hunt us down
with salty licks and unpaid bills, the dim
light of romance can kill our will.

I want him to read the paper I will
present on sex talk with couples that get sexy,
do it without condoms, with the lights dim,
while people like me tell them the boring
details. I can't get this part down
and simply listen to the mandolin.

You want me to be the mandolin
and play myself at will,
the papered academic who lies down
with theory and pretends it's sexy
as she peels banana-flavored condoms like it were a bore:
I want to tell him to stay that sexy man
who will ride me into thunderstorms
while I bore down the dim talk of this.

My Feminist Valentine

And when you have forgotten your birthday party,
the cocktails that churned your stomach like a polluted lake
and most especially when you have forgotten our tired talk,
how you blurted "let's just get married," a curled question (in bed).
My queries about marriage always unfolded in bed.
    Notice gag straddles the middle of enGAGement?
    Can bisexual feminists be married and be feminist?
Or the fun of not telling how we shacked up
after the lure of my Moroccan food, couscous scented
with the triumphant cilantro, turmeric, and cinnamon,
any food after hours of sex and philosophy in bed
for the love of my pet rat who lapped latte foam, mornings
we snuck to work with different routes to confuse
and keep love cool. And if we forget the question
from the bored court clerk who missed our smirks
how we both held our names with strong hands,
the legal wedding Monday at the criminal courthouse
planned over a delicious weekend;
the call to our friends, the cheap silver rings,
grocery store bouquet tied with gold ribbon,
new skirt, shirt and pants, the receipts pinned into our album.
Then recall the real wedding, the love we cemented
in Madrid where only voices were required to wed,
vows penciled on paper and read with squinted eyes on the edge
of the park, too dark to wander in further.

Painting the Church-House Doors Harlot Red on Easter Weekend

My good people of the Midwest walk-by
with their kids and dogs properly leashed
while I paint the doors of my church
Red. And by red, I mean the kind of red
you dream of on the day your husband is diagnosed
with cancer, when your child screams in red
because the only thing you can do
is make coffee, keep appointments, do the daily
things that hold you together. Red shouts
welcome if you believe in Feng Shui
and gave a place to stay in earlier American times,
though I prefer the Scottish idea of paid-off-mortgage-red
and superstitious church folk's screw-off-evil-red,
a place you want to take-off-your-shoes red.
When you live in a once church, the *door as mouth* metaphor
means there is no other color to decorate a door;
red means you manage the messy art of containment.

Memo to Faulkner from the Fluff and Fold

"Assumptions lie behind the work ..."
Richard Hugo, The Triggering Town

Dear Sandra, you know poets still believe
in hand-crafted words, write slowly in pen
on blank pages with spiral bound notebooks
lifted from the coffee shop next to school.
They never write in pen because it seeps
like a grease stain on the twelfth revision.
Poets sit in empty rooms, make it up.
They write on screen about their successful affairs
talk for hours about the failed ones
make mothers weep with all that blasphemy.
Listen Faulkner, you must fold poems like sheets
think in iambs for hours without sleep
take a crayon and scribble it all out.
Wait for weeks, the words will tumble in dreams
to the mind's ridiculous arenas.
That is how the writing is done. XOXO, Dick.

Stubborn @ Dinner

Mom: If you don't eat your dinner, you are not getting ANYTHING else to eat tonight.

Mimi: I don't want dessert. Yay, no dessert for me. I'm EXCITED about no dessert.

Mom: And, you get to eat your dinner for breakfast, too.

Mimi: Can I have what you have for breakfast?

Mom: I'm having coffee.

PURL STITCH

through the loop on the left needle

pull the loop

in front

with the yarn

Girl Bravado

Mimi: I am four, so I can lift a dinosaur.

Mimi: Now that I am four, I can do this.

Mimi: Now that I am four, I like cream cheese.
Four year olds like cream cheese.
When I was three, I didn't like it.

Mimi: My friend, the baby, will talk when she is four.
Because four year olds are kids.

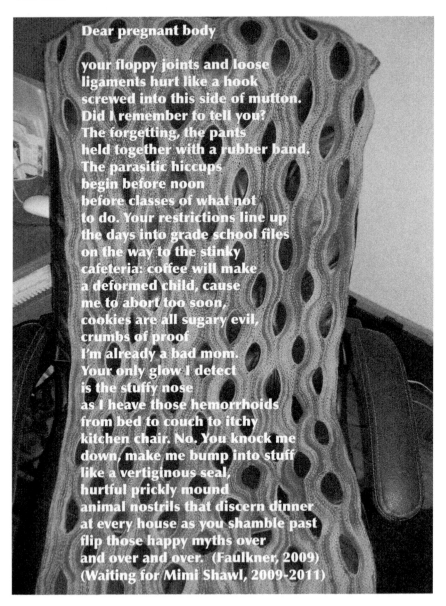

Dear pregnant body

your floppy joints and loose
ligaments hurt like a hook
screwed into this side of mutton.
Did I remember to tell you?
The forgetting, the pants
held together with a rubber band.
The parasitic hiccups
begin before noon
before classes of what not
to do. Your restrictions line up
the days into grade school files
on the way to the stinky
cafeteria: coffee will make
a deformed child, cause
me to abort too soon,
cookies are all sugary evil,
crumbs of proof
I'm already a bad mom.
Your only glow I detect
is the stuffy nose
as I heave those hemorrhoids
from bed to couch to itchy
kitchen chair. No. You knock me
down, make me bump into stuff
like a vertiginous seal,
hurtful prickly mound
animal nostrils that discern dinner
at every house as you shamble past
flip those happy myths over
and over and over. (Faulkner, 2009)
(Waiting for Mimi Shawl, 2009-2011)

Pacifier Ode

next to the shiny
cans priced with promise
for smart growth,
super powered limbs,
beside the temperature
sensitive spoons, sippy cups
bibs with cartoon faces—
things you never thought to need—

presides the paci, dummy, baby
comforter, all soother
silicone or rubber nub,
earlier a knot of fabric
soaked with the good stuff,
the thing you said no
to before you knew
the bite of attachment parenting

before the cry that broke
your single will, before
the warmth of plastic, sucking
like a fetus, like a magician
that bends objects beyond
what's possible
to this two-dimension time and space,
unnatural body that's better
than a fleshy nipple

Instructions for Surviving Infant

Remember the stubborn latch
clown purple mouth of gentian violet
your own face melted off
from exhaustion, say no thanks
to the OB at the 6 week cry
because you must remember
remember not to have another
do not get over it
do not cherish this
no taking something to ease your face
all ears that ear plugs can't stop up.

Forget which onesie you put
on the 9 week old you have to pick up,
panic when you must identify her
on the floor in the infant room
because all the white babies look alike,
rows of drool encrusted chins
clumsy arms in the nursery.
Don't tell them her first sentence:
Daddee needs more beer.

Over-Active Letdown

My super power means
even lactation consultants
are not safe from the arch of spray,
pure power, pure stubborn,
no bonding here
you contested and I persisted
like daughter like mother,
give away the parent manuals,
offer no cloak of citations.

When I was 7 weeks old
I went back to teach, to speed up
the insufferable infancy,
the mothering work I suck at.
Sit your boots in the chair
Baby Doo, Ms. Baby.
First words: *dog, ball, ockpuss.*
Other first sentence: *More cookie, please.*

How to Potty Train when Presenting a Manuscript on Maternal
Poetry

Drink a cold espresso after the coffee line maul.
Catch the conference plane with a wet crotch in your pants.
Think about how you are not a (fill in the blank) mom.

Don't speak of tiny fish crackers, too much
starch and big T-truth makes them antsy,
like a double espresso day line at the mall.

Walk with dry pants to the podium, blink like a mole
fresh from under the school, that darkened land
where we all crawl with bloody knees to this mom

they all want you to be. Now with malice,
No, no,   No, do not pant.
Drink that espresso, man.

If you must answer that question about your mind
the biography behind your paper, the argument in the last part
Repeat: "but I am no star mother"

as you curl your fingers by the podium mums
yellowed from the incandescent lights, you can't
ignore the conference attendees' espresso mad,
say, "I don't want to be your mommy."

Middle-Aged Run

You know you are middle aged
when the mist at the top of the hill
on your run beside the brook
burping over lichen caressed rocks
makes you slip; lost footing
on the urbane nature trail,
faux wood planks crank
your 20 year-old plantar fasciitis,
widen the leak in your pelvic floor
make you sure you are the blood mobile
all urine and sweat and smelly fluids.
You know where every porta-potty
sits and urinate in daylight
in front of the elementary school
where you daughter learns
because you won't unload
in your pants, down your ankles.
You know that it gets
better after the fourth mile,
but all you can think is this:
what a serial killer view,
if I stop to pee in front of a tree
who will be waiting?
The most dangerous thing to do
is run alone with all of this age.

Mother/Daughter

it = putting on shoes, spilling ovaltine into a glass of milk
this = eating blueberries with a toothpick
that = jumping off any object that leaves a bruise like a rainbow egg

The Daughter
Age 1: me
Age 1.5: Mimi do it.
Age 2: I do it.
Age 2.3: I want to do it!
Age 3: Someday Mimi will show you how to do this.
Age 3.3: Someday, Mom, when you are older,
I will show you how to do this.
Age 3.5: I will show you how to do that sometime.
You can't do that. Only I can do that.
Age 3.6: Say it!

The Mother
@15: date the bad boy
named the III after too many patriarchs,
the one with the curls, dirt bike, car,
sneak out with a short skirt
then say no. Say it
@19: alone on a train,
two weeks of European solitude,
five days of travel caked on your teeth
tramped into the socks you no longer wash
in sinks or tubs at hostels, rented rooms,
train stations. Ride alone.
Sit on a bench outside
the Alte Pinakothek, reek
with 19 year old girl-bravado,
make a proper Municher sniff
and take leave, your smell
like an effluvium of personal safety.
Talk to a stranger from Canada,

share strawberries out of a paper cone
after you shower for the first time
in five days, talk for the first time,
Say sorry
@27: to the sad scientist,
his disapproval of your desire
your writing, your move
states away for your job
your new lady love.
Say too bad
@29: and break up with the woman
for the too old artist
and drinking, driving, poetry—
especially the poetry.
Do it
@32: cheat on the poet-artist
with your new lust
cum love, who loves you
like a slow moving cancer
Say that
@41: screw the high school memories
that rain on your head
as you run alone
along the only green path
that snakes through the suburban sprawl
that ate your childhood. Run alone;
this is the most dangerous thing
your middle-aged bravado can do.

Baby Ripple Blanket

How many did you make, mom, your busy hands
always at my back like a rat weaving a nest
of old shirts, unwashed laundry, stolen domestic detritus?

You knit to ease time, your needles ignored
the summer practices, winter and spring recitals
your sweaters and blankets, offerings

to those who nagged you. My whiskers too long
curled in the air of an open car window
when you gunned the finned Buick as if the streets

were the tracks of a subdivision roller coaster, your hands
the restraints. I was a nubile pup, still nestled in
the passenger seat, eyes sewn over with pink skin,

waiting for you to drop the treat, hands like paws
a gentle scratch on my cheek to remind me
to ravel and unravel stupid youth.

1975 Singer *Athena 2000* Electronic Sewing Machine

I. Crafting with Grammy

I remember drives woven over the central PA hills
through fog like cotton candy and senility
to the suburbs of Philly,
the place where my now southern mother
saw puberty, and I see graduate school,
you and your sewing machine
that cost a fortune even then,
the first electronic machine for a woman
who learned to sew with a dead dad
and stepmother who never remarried
but thought Huey was the man
for you because of money, money.
(You chose the redheaded Lyle instead).
You lived with Emily D and "Auntie" Lou
the dressmaker who never married,
her engagement shot dead with a beau in WWII;
the ease of crafting your talent with a full flush of women,
your older sister and two half-sisters *not worth your little pinky*
as you visited the other mother, the real Theresa
and her memories of watching from the edge,
you and your sisters play in the park.

II. The Conversation

Sandra: I don't want children.

Grammy: Who is going to take care of you
when you get old?

Sandra: I don't want to get married, either.

III. The Advice

Stitch passive aggressive knots
into blankets, bathrobes and booties.
Say thank you for the money
crumpled into your hand after a visit
because people only give what they want.
When you get up at 5 am to bake cupcakes
for preschool or teacher appreciation day
because the ones from last night burnt,
use frosting to cover any blemishes
and never say *my mistake*;
mean it with no regrets.
Always be in charge of the money
and never record in a ledger
what you actually have in an account.
When a man is angry, cackle at him from a distance
in the attic with the stairs drawn up and door shut,
your voice only an echo through the house.

Dinner @ the Church-House with the 4-year-old

Mom: Stop belching, Mimi. If I get a report from preschool that you were burping during lunch to make your friends laugh, I will be irritated.

Dad: Stop. Mimi.

Mimi: I could barf on my plate if I keep burping, right?

Dad: And then you would have to eat your food with the barf.

Mimi: How many more bites do I have to eat to have dessert?

HURDLE STITCH

Cast on an odd number of stitches (CO 25 sts.)

Row 1: Knit, Right Side (K) (RS)
Row 2: Knit, Wrong Side (K) (WS)
Row 3: Knit 1, Purl 1 (K1, P1 across)
Row 4: Knit 1, Purl 1 (K1, P1 across)

REPEAT ROWS 1-4

Row 1: (K) (RS)
Row 2: (K) (WS)
Row 3: (K1, P1 across)
Row 4: (K1, P1 across)
Row 1: (K) (RS)
Row 2: (K) (WS)
Row 3: (K1, P1 across)
Row 4: (K1, P1 across)
Row 1: (K) (RS)
Row 2: (K) (WS)
Row 3: (K1, P1 across)
Row 4: (K1, P1 across)
Row 1: (K) (RS)
Row 2: (K) (WS)
Row 3: (K1, P1 across)
Row 4: (K1, P1 across)
Row 1: (K) (RS)
Row 2: (K) (WS)
Row 3: (K1, P1 across)
Row 4: (K1, P1 across)
Row 1: (K) (RS)
Row 2: (K) (WS)
Row 3: (K1, P1 across)

Row 4: (K1, P1 across)
Row 1: (K) (RS)
Row 2: (K) (WS)
Row 3: (K1, P1 across)
Row 4: (K1, P1 across)
Row 1: (K) (RS)
Row 2: (K) (WS)
Row 3: (K1, P1 across)
Row 4: (K1, P1 across)
Row 1: (K) (RS)
Row 2: (K) (WS)
Row 3: (K1, P1 across)
Row 4: (K1, P1 across)
Row 1: (K) (RS)
Row 2: (K) (WS)
Row 3: (K1, P1 across)
Row 4: (K1, P1 across)
Row 1: (K) (RS)
Row 2: (K) (WS)

Row 3: (K1, P1 across)
Row 4: (K1, P1 across)
Row 1: (K) (RS)
Row 2: (K) (WS)
Row 3: (K1, P1 across)
Row 4: (K1, P1 across)
Row 1: (K) (RS)
Row 2: (K) (WS)
Row 3: (K1, P1 across)
Row 4: (K1, P1 across)
Row 1: (K) (RS)
Row 2: (K) (WS)
Row 3: (K1, P1 across)
Row 4: (K1, P1 across)
Row 1: (K) (RS)
Row 2: (K) (WS)
Row 3: (K1, P1 across)
Row 4: (K1, P1 across)

Bind off all stitches loosely (BO all sts.)

Nietzsche @ the Coffee Shop

Mimi: Are Jesus and God dead?

Dad: I can't answer that.

Mom: (giving a "really?" look to Josh) It depends on whether you think they were people. If Jesus was a person, then yes. God is more of an idea.

Mimi: (pretend reading from a book) Jesus and God died in a terrible storm. A tornado killed them. Strong winds made them die.

Mom: Okay.

Mimi: (singing) I love Jesus. I hate God. I love God. I hate Jesus. Who killed God?

Mom: Nietzsche.

Learn to Knit

Cast on an odd number of stitches (CO #? sts)

on the drive to the family farm
with a consult from a hip stitch book
after only watching grandmother's needles,
your mother's needles stitch out

vests and sweaters and blankets.
Decrease for the dead,
mourn as you knit a row
wrap a stitch, quit your English method

for the fancy continental style
of pick with stick because it makes
a college girl chic crafty.
Learn to purl on a camping trip

with a husband everyone wanted
for you. Do not be too wrapped
with short rows to the past
read only the obits, the dead classmates

like a moth-eaten baby sweater,
change unraveling your cool.
Stop resisting the needles and wool
because it is too hard, too feminine

remember your grandmother
by buying dresses with pockets
to keep Ziplocs sealed with cigarette butts,
coffee candy, too clumsy to knit them yourself.

Bind off all stitches loosely (BO all sts).

CHAPTER 1

Telemarketers

When they call me I feel rage, say I'm not
at home and laugh at my cleverness,
the fact that we both know I'm there
and lying. But they do not call me on it

though they dial my number. Sometimes
they ask for my husband. I say sorry no spouse
here, but what I really mean is he can't talk right
now. I drag my husband and kids behind me

in a house, chain them to the peach tree in the backyard.
The scene where I fatten them up with butter beans, grits
and domestic bliss makes me crawl on my back
and shake without stop. I say no to the daily

paper and new credit, but now the solicitors
outwit me when they call me by name,
make me think I should recognize their voice
like my old lover who used that tone they day

I told him to get out. Their voices on the line
mirror his familiar ring that wore away
the silver lining of my escape plan. I almost
whip it out and give them my account numbers,

but I hang up before they reveal their wares,
my tongue no longer sweet as muscadines.
He argues that I've become mean and hard
like a New Yorker, that I need to find somewhere

in between then and now. But the boxes they check,
the scripts they read, tighten around me like a noose
because to listen is to agree, to bend in the wind
of all that talk. I ask them what they think

of phone plans, revolving credit, really think about paperback books and alumni like me who kick their shins
with hard-soled shoes before they call my chicken,
before I can tell them it's Dr. and not Mrs.

Pretty Straight Girls

Don't hold hands with women when they smell
of sweat, urine and tears. They don't like the taste of salt

between thigh-gap that does not exist,
the idea of those thighs as a pillow for sex.

They don't write dirty things in their minds
or diaries about their new female colleague,

don't notice her short filed finger nails
the flecks of yellow in her brown butch eyes

and make up reasons to take her to NYC
and then flirt with purpose while still dating a man.

They don't crave their knuckles to be warm
inside her like a duck opening its bill.

They probably pretend that her touch is safe
that she can't tattoo bisexual all over their breasts.

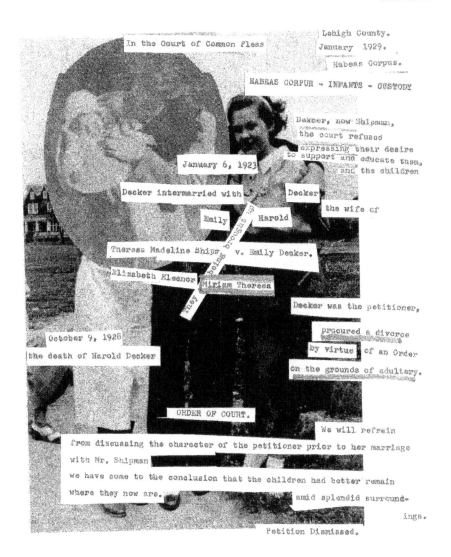

In the Court of Common Pleas

Lehigh County.

January 1929.

Habeas Corpus.

HABEAS CORPUR - INFANTS - CUSTODY

Decker, now Shipman,
the court refused
expressing their desire
to support and educate them,
and the children

January 6, 1923

Decker intermarried with   Decker

the wife of

Emily   Harold

Theresa Madeline Shipm   v. Emily Decker.

Elizabeth Eleanor   Miriam Theresa

They being brought up

Decker was the petitioner,

procured a divorce

by virtue of an Order

on the grounds of adultery.

October 9, 1928

the death of Harold Decker

ORDER OF COURT.

We will refrain
from discussing the character of the petitioner prior to her marriage
with Mr. Shipman
we have come to the conclusion that the children had better remain
where they now are.   amid splendid surround-

ings.

Petition Dismissed.

Faulkner's Furious Tank

She rides it hard
brandishes a war banner
fashioned from female condoms,
IUD's and Plan B, strung out
like a scarf to refract rainbows
in the court-appointed conformist slit
eyes that follow Faulkner as she trolls streets
stationed atop a purple tank
flanked by the fem squad,
just a pinch of yankee hostility
thrown in with sharp needles
to knit and crochet the revolution.
The squad rests their bloody boots
on the politician's shrinking
mahogany as Faulkner throws arms
and crafted uteri at the dissed
and franchised girl power,
toys that leave pink powder
marks on small strong hands.

Hoagland Writes to Faulkner about Thingitude
 —for Tony Hoagland

Your idea of poems as constructed lines,
collisions between research and aesthetics
reminds me of a stack of metaphors—
a poem equals language plus attention
thought so hard it cracks the sugared pavement—
I woke up with something else in my mind,
poets playing hockey on Nascar tracks,
critics skating with black and white jerseys
kicking ice chips with dull blades on banners
for tacos, children's hospitals, and banks.
Faulkner, tell how to stop the fracture
of poetics over the brass bars, how
to choose the war soaked news without boozy
critique? Tell me how to put myself back to bed.

Dead Leg Ode

I. Where is Pop-Pop's leg?

My daughter asks what
we all want to know.
Think of Merleau-Ponty, how
this sounds like an existential question,
but this is not phenomenology
this is practical like
What did they do with it?
What do you do
with an amputated leg?
Burn it in the hospital oven,
throw it in the river,
take it for a spin down
a hall, through the waiting room
until you get to the dead leg dance.
Will my leg get sick?
We all think of this,
how some legs need
to be released
from bodies, tired
of inefficiencies
cut to a stump.
How many legs do you have?
Does the stump
count as a limb
chopped off after
the storm of failed surgeries?

II. With two legs on the way to the package store to buy a keg:

Dad: The doctor asked me what I had been doing
      to get my numbers down.

Daughter: What did you tell him?

Dad: I told him I switched to light beer. He asked,
      "How much beer do you drink a day?"

Daughter: (inaudible) (Laugh).

Dad: I told him a gallon. (Smirk). (Laugh).

Daughter: And?

Dad: He told me to keep doing what I was doing.

III. Stump Management

This is what it is called
when you lose a leg:
the stump needs exercise
needs you to manage
the swell and shrink of incision
needs you to stump for
a political walk.

Don't ask the physical therapist
where to get a cup holder,
riding the wheelchair while
drinking a cold one
is not managing.
Shove the stump into a prosthetic,
manage your fear
of a fall.

Bedtime Story
   "Guys, don't eat the moon in space and in the clouds."
                                    -Mimi, age 2
 What's going on at Mimi's house?

the bears bite
     the bed off
the bears bite
     the room off

I don't want to bite
     the bears because
because they
are too strong

Why do the walls hatch?

All the raspberries fall
     down my throat

I want a Manhattan

Doing Dishes

If you put me
    in the dishwasher,
I will melt.
I will turn
    into a dish, someday.
Then we
will be
in the hunger line.

At the Viewing

Mimi: Who is that?
Mom: That's Grandma Helen.
Mimi: Is she old?
Mom: Yes.

Helen presides from her casket, salon coiffed hair, cheeks like gas station roses waxed too much to eat, some suit we never saw her wear pressed against satin. We are here to show the town how we keep our kid alive: watch her ninja-snake under the pews, slide past the folding metal chairs, crawl around the paneled divider that keeps grief separated into rooms. She wants none of this adult time, spits on a neighbor when she wants a hello, refuses to make an apology, buttons her eyes shut. We don't talk about death; don't explain to our three year old what happens after the party. She dumps the limp roly poly from the Mason jar outside on the still-attached grass to resuscitate its life. Months later, the hangover caught up with us on a walk with the dog. A dead squirrel on the street, the pavement drunk on its fluids, carcass smashed into two dimensions, intestines squirting out its flat mouth. Next the questions from the child's mouth, the ones with impossible answers: Will the squirrel be alive tomorrow? Why is there a dead squirrel on Maple Street? Death means a squirrel with heart squeezed through mouth visible to the dogs and children while cars continue driving over our conversation.

Guns @ Breakfast

Mimi: Can I stay home? I don't wanta go to school today.

Mom: No. Mom and Dad have to work. Though, we could leave Buddy in charge, and you could stay here.

Mimi: He's not a human.

Mom: True, but he would tell you if anyone was outside.

Mimi: He would bark at strangers.

Mom: We'd lock the door, and then you would know not to answer it.

Mimi: But what if they broke the door down? I would run away.
I would take a sword and stab them.
But they would have a gun.

FROGGING

to "rip it, rip it"

the

unraveling

of
knitting
mistakes

Morning Coffee

Mimi: When you and dad die when I am an adult, I won't mind because I will do my own stuff.

Mom: Will you be sad?

Mimi: I will live in this house with my baby.
Will Buddy be sad when you die?

Mom: Let's hope he dies before me. Dogs shouldn't live that long.

Mimi: I don't like blood. Does blood come out of dead bodies?

In this breaking up dream

your right foot sticks in a flaming
suitcase, orange and red sparks
burn the base of our bed, rented
in some Victorian on University Hill.
I fall off a decrepit chair
mid-lecture, clutch your spitting
pet parrot who has always hated me,
notice charred clothes and consonants
transform into constant aches when magic
markers refuse to write on your skin
or dry erase boards made of hamster pelts.

You can't help me get unstuck,
even the coffee steamed in my cup
as I start the week can't take
the black soot smell away
make me grateful for your love notes
tucked away in my computer annex.

Writing a Cancer Sonnet @ the ENT Doctor's Office, December 4, 2013

If you have to have a type of cancer,
this is what you want: I roll these words with my tongue
suck this pity platitude because someone
has to steer the car home, ask for answers,
ask my husband if he needs to sit down.
   He is sitting down, diagnosed the doc:
But I see his color slide from forehead to socks
the whitewash of fear like a tainted toy clown.
I apply the lipstick of a smile and the wife role
to write the tasks of what to do with hands so cold.
I make a pot of coffee, pour in a slug
from our dusty liquor rack of love
as we sit, dark on the couch, with the old
dog thinking our thoughts of too much
                         holding.

Death and Dying

Mimi: Why will Back in the Day not come again?

You do the good parent
make opportune conversations
like the crunch of a healthy breakfast
part of the day, tell the kid
that her namesake Miriam
the first, and her great,
is dead: *Why will Dead Miriam*
not crochet any more bed dolls?

You respond to the question
with that right answer;
Dead means turning
into earth for worm tunnels
becoming something else. But
like most parenting it is not enough:
Will I die someday? Will you die?
Will Buddy die? Will daddee
die, will, willwillwillwill—

We can be a useful aesthetic;
You talk about trees,
how we turn into dirt
that can grow vegetables
like cauliflower and beets
and perky flowers,
purple and pink: *I don't*
want to turn into dirt.
Is Grandma that tree?
I don't want to be a tree.

But humanism fails you
at bedtime, in the car-seat,
all those God-Less spaces

where words like myths
can't make it pretty: *I don't want to die/*
I don't want to die/I don't want to die/ I don't want to die/
I don't want to die/I don't want to die/

Millicent's Opera Glasses

"We can't lie and say we have somewhere to go tomorrow, so we'll
be here all night ...We're not leaving here until I finish this bottle of
wine."
—Eddie Vedder, Pearl Jam Concert, State College, Pennsylvania,
May 3, 2003

I. Act One

I focus in on my altar, collect stares
from the college males as I use
the mother of pearl and brass
scroll-work opera glasses.
You complain about the seats
too far away from the stage
while they pretend not to watch me
watch them spit liquor off
our choir seats, wipe the wetness off
chins with torn cuffs like small kids.
Great grandmother Millie must
have used these glasses cum binoculars
between her own classical piano tours.
I hope she snuck in sherry or vermouth,
calculated modified stage dives off
upper box seats into a writhing unctuous crowd.

II. Act Two

I smile at the not so secret smoke
handed around. Security stops and scolds
the ones who just now found the art
of being bad. We exchange high fives
that just miss, hit me in the gut.
Millie's glasses passed hand to hand
like a flask, I wonder if she craved
the crowds and claps she surrendered
for the Scottish salesman and the wife-
tour through blue collar Philly,
gas refineries and electric pole climbing.
You play the petulant partner now
as I surrender our apartment
for my new job somewhere else,
without you.

III. Act Three

I lost my best friend last tour, wet
on a split garbage bag, cheap grass seats
suspended in some half-way zone,
Trenton or Philly? We sipped free beer
tabled for a good tip. "Your white friends
treat me like a fresh-air fund kid."
Ed flaunts green jeans, worked-out biceps,
all we feel is sex, and hear is sex,
when he rolls up his sleeves.
Sing with me he purrs; teachers leave those kids alone,
but kids, don't leave those politicians alone.
I can't know that this is another break-up
as we sit and sip our crappy beer,
so I play the teacher who needs to lick the sweat
that pools like the Susquehanna in the hollow
of his throat; I grip the binoculars, drown
like a randy pirate who worships lust.

Relational Therapy

My friend makes me imagine dating myself
so I know what my exes know:

I could fuck and not make
a relational statement. My network

of one would never require a plan,
no dates to mark on the calendar,

no need for talk
about talk or apologies.

The day we ended it I lit up
the secret pack of smokes

to feel young and angry. If I were my own
lover, I could remain silent about feelings

because I would know what I intended to say
would be. If I were my own lover, I could

ignore the sighs and gripes about young girls
whose tastes shift like smoke rings in the wind.

At the end, she took her bed from the basement
but not me, orange rust framed my hands,

but if I were my own lover, I would
breathe words in without tasting blood

I would make all the rules. I would
make all of the rules.

How to Write a Break-Up (#2)

Pretend you don't notice
the ink of her new tattoo or
the thud of his terry cloth shorts

as he drops them in front of you
on the floor of the new studio
you visit because you're friends now,

and friends undress in front of friends.

Take note of the names hurled
at you because you quit it, the jilter-
fake-lesbian-couscous-eater

little girl, ruined by feminism, fallen.
Spill your red wine on their white carpet
while making large gestures.

Always be the one to break it off:
leave him for her and then her for him,
be a non-discriminate leaver.

Sing the break-up story
with the malice of righteousness,
no more limping and wilted words.

You ended the tired thing
with your own words
because they wouldn't.

Forget the scars from sledding
accidents, the curve of ass
the taste of sweat like half-sour pickles

parts you traced with intimate fingers.

Rip up the fed-exed note
delivered to work in front of friends
declaring you better than a Pearl Jam song.

How to Date Catholic Boys

Talk about premarital sex
like a summer baseball game
to attract the devout.
Paste lipstick kisses on
his stomach instead of Hail Marys.
Use confession to exorcise your
body out of his holy virgin thoughts.
Genuflect over cheap beer in bars
where men wear ties to play pool
and seduce women with alcohol and arguments,
rituals polished like communion cups.
Use left-over cell minutes to break it
off because you want to be the whore.
Memorize these rituals with practice.
Repeat. Order another beer
and touch his knee. Repeat.

RearViewMirror

> —After RVM by Pearl Jam and with a line from Kim Addonizio

Once you airmailed me a jar of jam from the yard
where we had lived together when I believed

in the lilies blooming in the black vase,
once I saw those Pennsylvania blackberries, jarred

in a Madrid café when I was months married
to the man you anticipated I would screw

and who would not suffer for desperate love like us,
I imagined we had lasted, our faces flushed,

sweat like fear, sticking us to the seats in your blue van.
I saw things, saw things clearer when eating

dry toast, starved after sex in some other rented room.
How could you know I saw you in the rear view mirror?

Cleaning out the Sock Drawer

The thigh highs strangle the knee-highs
waxy wool caught between slippery silk,
all her past snags like fabric over-dyed.

She pulls out a spare sock that lies,
a fuzzy reminder of some younger ilk.
The thigh-highs strangle the knee-highs

and she can't untangle all the goodbyes,
who bought her panties the color of milk
all the past snags like funky fabric over-dyed.

The gothic grosgrain bows stop her shy
that romp and roll with an artist in the grassy hills
where her thigh-highs strangled his knee-highs

and then the pubic pink fishnets, pried
off her legs after a dramatic driveway spill.
All her past snags like fabric over-dyed.

She puts on a pair of trashed thigh-highs
knit with bamboo needles by her mom, still
her thigh-highs strangle the knee-highs
all the past snags like fabric over-dyed.

Death @ Bedtime

Mimi: Where did my great-grandmother die?

Mom: In Pennsylvania.

Mimi: Why?

Mom: That is where she lived.

Mimi: How did she die, my great-grandmother who I am named for?

Mom: She died in her apartment. She was tired. May we all get to choose like that how we want to die.
Your dad's grandmother, May, died in Missouri.

Mimi: Did Miriam who died in her apartment, die with her tongue, stick-out?

KITCHENER STITCH

graft   L   together

            I

                V

                    E

                        stitches

an*invisible*join

Date Nut Muffins @ Breakfast

Mimi: If I eat all of my breakfast, after school, can I have chocolate?

Mom: No. You eat all of your breakfast so you can grow and get older and do all of those things you keep asking about like sliding down the big water slide at the park.

Mimi: But I don't want to grow. Growing gives me leg cramps.
By the way, I will eat lunch and snack at school and grow.
And more snack after school.
And I get to take a nap, and you don't.

Home, Run

Flash Faulkner remembers
19 and teenage boy fear
splashed in cologne rivers
that run through the high school
morning fog that chokes.
The home run is here
where you never tire
of the look of light
on buildings that change
only for you, your feet
move here without prompt
in familiar rhythms.

Invitation to a Dead Grandmother

It's happy hour, Dear Miriam,
I want you to come meet us
drink in our church-house
play hangman with the kid,
the game that seems like toddler talk
    the missing prepositions
who needs all of those words?

Notice your barren worries for me
squirm well after your death:
knitting needles wrapped with vests
cookie butter soft on the counter
child organized cabinets
with cans of trout and oysters lined like a bus
service by size from oven to altar.

I would pour you a fresh bourbon or scotch
cask strength and uncut like in the old days
splash in some pretend soda,
a toast to the child with your name,
the one you told me I needed.
It's (always) cocktail hour here
at our house, the church of the petulant parrot:
    I want _ Manhattan.

Ignore the impatient mommy-words that snake
down the drain at bath time,
the curtains sewn with crooked hem
because the (damn) tension is screwed
on your bequeathed machine,

notice the kid's first word,
your post-children hobby,
under the kitchen table as he vomits
fur balls of anxiety with crusty food

after the ():
    I don't wanta bite the bears
       _ _ _ _ _ _ _they are too strong.

Lament

Dad: I just can't hold as much beer as I used to.

At our "not wedding" party,
Dad bought the keg for the beer drinkers
because wine is for wimps
and prissy college professors
who get married at the criminal courthouse
and then throw some party
a year and a month later
at a winery with a view
of just the slivered tip of a lake.
At the end of the night,
Dad lamented he *just couldn't
hold anymore*, the last pitcher
sweating on the winery counter.
And now with his right leg gone
on vacation with our family,
the biggest lament is his inability
to hold as much beer.

Bye-Bye Paci
Fall Break, Rustic Cabin, Hocking Hills

Mimi: Why did the people who clean the cabin throw away paci? (repeat)

Mom: That's their job.

Mimi: Why? Why? Why? WHY? Why? I want blue paci!

Mom: Maybe a lion ate it.

Mimi: Is it in his throat? I want it back. I hope he chokes.

ATKINSON DAIRY

Nanny Says

That's the price you pay
        for being beautiful as we color
        my hair the Sandy auburn of her fathers
        starting in pre-pubescent fifth grade.
That's the price you pay
        for being different, for the love
        of hand-me-down golf pants dizzy with plaid;
        fast pinches and your-so-ugly taunts
        the price paid in middle-school lines.
Nanny asks me if there are no men
        at school for me to date
        when I say no marriage and no kids.
Nanny tells me to stop being
        the most miserable pregnant woman,
        that's the price women pay
        for being in the sex war and getting shot at.
Nanny heard that my brother wrote on Facebook
        his daughter is so beautiful he will beat boys with sticks.
        "Grammy never told my sister and me we were beautiful;
        She always mentioned what was off,
        what flaw she saw
        like our slip was showing."
Nanny says that she's glad none of her kids are gay
        because the price is a harder life:
        Nanny wants me to *take it easy*—
        Don't work too hard.

A Man, A Woman, Penetration

But come on, let's unhinge this
dear image of fucking,

get it unstuck.
I got in trouble in poetry

class because I thought,
Kiss my beaded purse,

was clever slang for oral sex—
think twat or box or fur pie—

my students look outside the door
when I tongue these words

to see who may walk in.
For fun, for the final

I may ask them what can,
what will happen next?

Suicide Window, Toledo

What if we rode a snowplough
like a corporate tank, scraped
the sidewalk outside a city church?
Citizens riddled with snow shovels,
our angry boots coagulate sand,
the new urban detritus.
Beautiful branches erupt out of dead buildings,
the drone of the suburban engine
whines into wild city corners
beside the rust belt graffiti:
Stop the Man, You Suck
Stick kids stuck inside a crumbled façade,
bubbled lines sprayed on the shells of lost jobs.
What if we spilled our lattes, clutched
with mittened hands, maroon yarn
spun tight like our city obituaries,
let our stomachs sour with unease.
Bobble heads burst on work truck dashboards,
listen to the rumble beneath
the undulating hack of just enough,
pare down the winter whip
beat our heads until we stop.

Winter Run

I wish that I were this winter's bitch
as she smacks my cheeks to a rosacea red
slides jagged fingers under my shirt until I slip,
my mouth all stretched circle and tongue, agape.
She kisses my tendonitis with ice knuckles
so I cry a polar vortex of popsicle tears
that she slaps across my lashes like a brass buckle.
Though her morning breath abrades my corneas
I damn the counties snow emergencies,
double-knot my laces and swerve around downed cars
stretching and cracking plantar to please.
I know that I am this winter's bitch
as I skid, a pile of yellowed snow in a ditch.

Remodeling Dream

The poems you did not
could not, catch at night
when your child needs to sleep
curled in your armpit,
scamper like lost hamsters,
squeeze into the space between
the drywall and the world
where only the dog
can hear their scratching;
the high-pitched squeak
of trapped disappointment.

How to Write a Break-Up (#3)

She writes what she remembers.

You're like a tiny tumor, spontaneous growth
that inveigles her academic persona

makes her skip the prescreening of poor personality,
the cataloged essay of relational observations.

Instead she rides wedged into your crevice
without a helmet, eats fries sans ketchup,

you both smashed together
on the same side of the booth.

She writes of you, forgets the others—
a series of bad choices listed on paper.

She pretends the play worked, love
hung, rose uncontained by labels.

She misses still what she can't write;

how the fun became like the longest
and most boring February.

Story Time

Mimi: Let's play teacher.

Mom: I don't want to. I do that for a living.

Mimi: When you guys die (pointing to mom & dad), I am turning this place into a school. Then, I will read all of these books to the kids
(sweeping gesture to a book case in our church-house).

Mom: You sure have a lot of plans for when I'm dead.

Mimi: The kids will be happy.

POETIC INQUIRY EXERCISES:
HOW TO WRITE POETRY ABOUT FAMILY

Gathering and Generating Family Materials

The Appendix is stuffed with exercises designed to get you writing about family in verse, perhaps even writing with family members. I outlined the benefits to a poetic treatment of family stories in the preface, so my goal here is to have you think about, generate, and gather material that will help you to write poems that (re)story family. The exercises I offer detail versions of my procedures for creating many of the poems in the collection *Knit Four, Frog One*.

First, you will want to collect materials to use for the poetic inquiry exercises I present. The materials I used in constructing poems included:

1. *Family artifacts* (e.g., photos, birth and death certificates, recipes, knit blankets, sewing patterns, journals, letters, emails, Facebook posts, court documents, genealogy papers, baby shoes, scrapbooks);

2. *Interviews and informal conversations*
You can ask family members and friends about memories, artifacts, and documents you have. You can ask family members and friends about memories they have. You should write down these conversations for use as source material. For example, I asked my mother about family photos and documents that I inherited from her and my grandmother and made sure to take notes when I opened the box in her presence. I also asked about specific items, like letters and postcards when I sorted through it again looking for memory triggers and ideas for poems to write. I shared the collage poems I made with my mother and asked her for her reactions. You can ask family

members about the meaning, memory, and value of specific photos, letters, and stories. Take notes and revisit the notes when searching for raw material to use in poems.

You can interview family members and make transcripts of the interviews. You may want to keep a journal of conversations.

Here are some questions you can ask family members to collect more stories:

a. What is your most vivid childhood memory?
b. What do you remember about (fill in the blank) incident?
c. What was it like to grow up in (fill in the blank)?
d. Who was your best friend in elementary school? In high school?
e. What did you/do you think about school?
f. What is your favourite family ritual?
g. Who do you consider to be family? What makes a family?
h. What were some of your favorite things to do as a child? As an adolescent? As a young adult?
i. Describe a family vacation. What was memorable about the trip?
j. How did family talk about problems? How did your family talk about difference? Please give examples.
k. How did family deal with crises?
l. How did family express emotion (e.g., joy, concern, anger)?

3. *Memories*

You may wish to develop and elaborate on your own family memories. I like Carolyn Ellis's (1995) description of introspective sociology in her work, *Final Negotiations*. She describes writing about her partner's death and then revisiting journal entries multiple times to fill in details and remember feelings and conversations about life events. For your family poems, take notes and use any journal writing, letters, emails/texts/social media posts as writing prompts. I kept a poetry journal during this book project in which I wrote down ideas for poems. Then I went back to the ideas and filled in details that I remembered. For example, I wanted to write about crafting with my grandmother. I wrote down snippets of conversations that I recalled and filled in details during subsequent writing sessions. I looked at pictures from that time as well as sewing patterns and sewing material she gifted me to trigger memories.

Ways to generate material: If you need help with recollecting some family stories, dialogues, and/or identity themes, write answers to the following prompts.

- What is the most embarrassing thing that has ever happened to you?
- What is one of your earliest memories? What is the overriding emotion you attach to this memory?
- What is a moment you remember feeling you were unfairly treated?
- What are you most afraid of?
- What is one of your best memories?
- What is one of your worst memories?
- What makes you angry? Sad? Happy? Content?
- What are ten of your most favorite things?
- What are ten of your least favorite things?
- Have you told anyone in your family the answers to the questions above? Why or why not?
- What are some stories that your family tells (or does not tell) about members in the family? What are some stories they tell about those outside of the family (e.g., divorce, infidelity)?
- What does a family celebration look like? Sound like? Smell like?

The purpose of these questions is to have you think about family themes that tell you something about who you are as a family, what constitutes important ways of being in the world, and the values and preferred identities that constitute your family history.

4. *Research*
As a social scientist, I must add that research about family processes, forms and functions is also a valuable source of material. There are excellent journals that publish social science work on families (e.g., *Sex Roles*, *Journal of Social and Personal Relationships*; *Journal of Family Communication*; *Journal of Marriage and the Family*;

Journal of GBLT Family Studies; Personal Relationships; Psychology of Women). You can start with some of the academic journals I list. Search the journal for the topic of interest (e.g., gender roles in family). You can also use search functions in library databases with keywords of interest (e.g., family conflict, family secrets, LGBTQ family) to find research articles to help you conceptualize a family topic. There are also many excellent journalistic writings on family (e.g., work by Arlie Hochschild) that may help you. Make notes and highlight passages in the articles that are of interest to you.

You could take this research and add it into your poems like I suggest in the found poem/poetic transcription exercise below. I researched information about family secrets and talking about death and dying with children, for instance. Some of the other information you will notice is described in the preface as an introduction and contextualization to the poetry collection.

Discussion Questions

I offer the following discussion questions to use with *Knit Four, Frog One*:

1. What family themes do you notice in the poems? What overarching themes does each section (i.e., knit stitch, purl stitch, hurdle stitch, Kitchener stitch) contain? What do these themes suggest about family roles, family communication styles, family values, and definitions of family?

2. What does this collection tell you about family communication? What kind of family is depicted in *Knit Four, Frog One*? What communication patterns do you notice? How does communication help the family resist or adapt to outside forces and crises that arise?

3. Faulkner claims that *the poems present stories of confirmation and disconfirmation, humor as resilience and distraction, mothering as friendship and resistance to authority, craft as love, and love as useful work.* Do you agree with this? Why or why not? How do you see these themes?

4. What does telling family stories in poetry offer readers? What would telling the stories in prose change about the meaning?

5. Are there any stories that ethically should not be shared? How do ethics play a role in our telling of family stories? What are the ethical considerations of sharing family information and family secrets?

6. Are there any poems missing from this collection? What do you think is not talked about? Why? Would you add any poems? Why or why not?

7. What do you like about the "characters" in the poems? What do you dislike about the "characters" in the poems? Explain.

8. In many instances, we narrate particular life experiences where there is a rift between a real and ideal self, between the self and

society (Riessman, 1993). In what places do you see Faulkner narrating about rifts between the self and society, the real and ideal? What does this narrating accomplish?

9. Faulkner talks about the poetry in this collection as feminist resistance. What does this mean? How do you see feminist ideas in play in the poems? What does it mean to be a feminist mother and partner?

10. Faulkner wrote in the introduction, "The social scientist turned to poetry as I had done during other stressful times in my life." What does it mean to claim poetry as social science? How does a poetic social science add to or detract from understanding of family and family communication?

Exercise I: Collage Poem (aka Cento)

Choose an interview or interviews to (re)present, a family story, research literature, and/or family theme (e.g., strength) to present in a collage poem.

Material to Use: interview transcripts, photos, field notes, letters, email, texts, researcher journal, research memos, crayons, pencils, pens, paint, double-sided tape, glue, family artifacts, yarn, magazines, cardboard, metals, fibers, recycled objects

Technique: photo-shop, cut and paste, installation, craft boxes, painting, fiber art, drawing

Background: A collage is a "gluing together" of elements. A cento is a poetic form that is made up of passages from more than one poet; it is a mixture or pastiche of poetic excerpts. In our present understanding, the cento is an intertextual form, "a barrage of quoted fragments" (Drury, 2006, p. 55). The power of collage rests in the potential for double meanings as Majore Perloff (e.g., http://marjorieperloff.com/stein-duchamp-picasso/collage-poetry/) writes:

> For each element in the collage has a kind of double function: it refers to an external reality even as its compositional thrust is to undercut the very referentiality it seems to assert. And further: collage subverts all conventional figure-ground relationships, it generally being unclear whether item A is on top of item B or behind it or whether the two coexist in the shallow space which is the "picture."

Alice Notley, a poet and visual artist, described how poetry and collage are interconnected in the autobiographical collection, *The Mysteries of Small Houses* (1998).

What is a poem   this
What is a poem   it's like a
Collage shapes in conjunction of
world and bright color

Version One: Found Poem/Poetic Transcription

Poetic transcription is a method of using poetry as/in research. Many researchers have eloquently discussed using poetic transcription as a way to enter into the world of the storyteller by preserving their speaking style and capturing the spirit of a story to portray its range of meanings (Madison, 1991, 2004), to make the shaping of stories more evident (Richardson, 2002), and to give "ownership of the words" to the speaker rather than the researcher (Calafell, 2004). A common method of poetic transcription entails researchers highlighting participants' exact words and language from interview transcripts, cutting and pasting the essential elements in an effort to reveal the essence of a participants' lived experience (Glesne, 1997). This works well with family interviews because you can preserve the style of the story telling.

Some researchers consider this process of extraction to be like found poetry; poetry that is created by using phrases, words, and passages from other sources such as newspaper articles, conversation, notes, lists, and even from email exchanges paying attention to spacing and/or line breaks. A found poem is a piece of writing that was not intended to be a poem but becomes one when the writer declares it one, having paid close attention to "exceptional uses of language or sharply presented, telegraphic stories that create a poetic effect or an emotional response as strong as that made by a poem" (Padgett, 1987, p. 82). The found poem represents writing/research that was not intended as poetry, but you will declare it such through your choice of "found" parts in your research. Padgett (1987) claims that one must only pay close attention to "exceptional" use of language, poetic stories, or those that create a strong affective response and decide on line-breaks and the poem's limits.

Walsh (2006) and Butler-Kisber (2002) both craft what they label found poems from interview data. Walsh (2006) described a process of reading transcripts many times while making notes and finding recurring themes. "I culled words and cut and pasted segments of conversation into specifically labeled files, then played poetically with the segments of conversation in an attempt to distill themes and write succinct versions of them" (p. 990). She reordered phrases to offer more clarity for the audience and made sure to include only those phrases that were important to an emerging theme. We used found poetry to bring us close to our relationship "data" and to use that relationship to bring different insight than a straightforward prose presentation would allow (Butler-Kisber, 2002).

You can represent the personal and relational identity themes in your family stories through the use of found poems/poetic transcriptions. I find this form to be an excellent way to present competing discourses because I adopt Young's (2010) position that poetry's strength is the ability to position dialectics. "A poem asserts itself as poetry by being in dialogue with what it resists" (p. 38).

How To: Use one or more interview transcript(s), journals, and/or literature from a project and:

Read a transcript and highlight words and passages that represent the interviewee and/or theme. You can use paper transcripts and cut the highlighted passages or you can collect the highlighted passages and cut and paste them in a word processing program. You may want to think about a theme you wish to represent in the work (e.g., family pride).

Arrange the highlighted words or cut-outs in a poem or poetic transcription that illustrates a theme, idea, or situation. Consider how line-breaks and enjambment can help the tension and sense of poetic language. As Drury (2006) noted, enjambment is key to "mark the rhythmic flow of a poem ... enjambment is like musical syncopation; instead of pausing, the musical phrase pushes ahead" (p. 93).

Version Two: Investigative Poem

This will be a form that can help you explore, question, and interrogate a family theme, story, and/or rule.

How To: Create an investigative poem by reading your transcripts, literature, journal, and notes, but don't read too closely (i.e., don't make any notes until AFTER you have read through the material a few times). Take notes, including phrases, quotes, and impressions after reading. Write a poem that includes: words that are important (what happened), your impressions and perceptions of what it was like, and connect the poem to a larger political context to show the personal and the historical intersection. This connection may be shown through the poem title or epigraph (e.g., Walker, 2008, 2013).

The poem "Dead Leg Ode" in this collection is an example. I created this poem to show how my family dealt with a health crisis. It demonstrates an indirect way of talking about difficult issues. It shows our culture's discomfort with disability. The italicized questions were my daughter's impossible to answer queries.

Version Three: Arts-Based Collage

Try creating a found poem using arts-based collage. This can be done in any medium that you are comfortable using (e.g., electronic, cut and paste, fiber arts, painting, sculpture, mixed media).

How To: Collect the material you wish to use in a collage. If you want to make a non-electronic collage, photocopy or make pdfs of important artifacts. Do a thematic analysis as described below in the poetic analysis exercise. Cut out the highlighted themes/important ideas. Cut out pictures that may be helpful. Think about how you could represent the theme/story you wish to present.

Lay out all of the pieces. Rearrange. Commit to your collage by gluing/using double sided-tape. Use any other material that helps you present the story/theme/idea (e.g., magazine pictures, fiber, recycled objects). You can make a pdf or take a picture of the collage. "my memories are mother" and "In the Court of Common Pleas" are examples of collage poems that I created from memories and ideas about family themes. I retold a story about mothering and origins based on court documents, family photos, and letters that I found in addition to the recollections I had about how my grandmother was adopted.

If you wish to use Photo-Shop, collect material in the same way. You can arrange photos of the material you wish and use the draw function. I did this with the poems "Bye-Bye Paci," "Waiting for Mimi," and "Bedtime Story." I had photos of my daughter's art, my knitting, and family that portrayed the themes of self-reliance, beauty, and loss that I wanted to explore in words and images.

Exercise II: The Dialogue Poem

This form will be well suited to interview transcripts and/or recollected conversations. I envision the dialogue poem like a post you often see presented in social media as a typical daily conversation. For example, all of the dialogue poems in Knit Four, Frog One are recreated from conversations between my daughter and me. Some of them I presented on my Facebook page in a similar form. Being a poet and a social scientist means that I pay attention to everyday conversation and details, listen for moments that resonate with me and larger cultural conversations, and may be opportunities for poem making (Rose, 1990).

How To: Recollect a conversation about a family story, theme, memory, and/or identity. Portray the memory using vivid dialogue (i.e. words, details, and scene that capture something important). After you have a dialogue, ask yourself how the dialogue represents the theme you wanted to portray? The theme may become the title of the poem. Share the dialogue with a family member or other and ask for their feedback. Write another dialogue poem based on feedback from the first poem. The poem title may be used to present the setting, the theme, or a feeling.

For example, the dialogue poem "Eating Dinner" in this collection represents the theme of family humor as way to contend with daily annoyances. The poem "At the Viewing" shows how you could use recreated dialogue. The poem re-presents a scene at Grandma Helen's viewing where I racked up parenting fail #315 because I did not talk about death with my then three-year old. I would like to say that my daughter and I had a deep conversation about death and dying after the viewing, that I was able to talk to my daughter in an age appropriate and snappy way. It was fall after all, a seemingly good time to talk about dying given the decay around. That moment passed, but we have been having numerous conversations since that time. These are moments I have presented in more dialogue poems you see in the current collection. They speak to the difficulty our culture has talking about death and dying.

Exercise Three: Poetic Analysis

One way to find themes in the interview transcripts/journals/family artifacts you have is to analyse the "data" like a social scientist. You may use a version of open coding akin to grounded theory where you review transcripts and materials line-by-line and make notes of descriptive codes, then use selective coding where descriptive codes are condensed and recategorized (Glaser, 1978). Rich Furman and colleagues have a good description of their process constructing research poems that may be of use (Furman, Lietz & Langer, 2006), and I have an article that details how I created found poems from a yearlong series of email exchanges that may also benefit your analysis (Faulkner & Ruby, in press).

How To:
1. Begin descriptive coding by reading your journals/ transcripts "searching for the essence conveyed, the hues, the textures, and then drawing from all portion of the interviews to juxtapose details into a somewhat abstract re-presentation" (Carr, 2003, p. 205). What this means is that you read through all of your materials to get a holistic sense of the data. Then consider the themes/ideas/concepts that you notice. You may wish to create a pdf file of your materials and analyze them using both on-line comment tools and by writing on paper copies of the document (e.g., highlighting words and phrases, making notes of categories and themes and theoretical memos with the sticky note function and writing in the margins). Ask yourself the following sensitizing questions as you read and reread your materials: "What does a listener need to know in order to render this textual segment intelligible? What socio-cultural and interpersonal discourses need to be invoked to understand what this textual segment means?" (Baxter, 2011, p. 159). Write down your initial impressions in the margins, noting answers to the question: "What is being said or implied about family identity?" (Baxter, 2011, p. 162).

2. Write a poem or poems about the themes using your coded material. The highlighted passages can become part of your poems. I

created the poem, "my memories are mother" based on my coding of family letters (a letter from my mother to her mother, notes and letters from my grandmother to me). The descriptive coding showed me the importance of mothering as friendship, and I cut out the portions of the letters that conveyed this theme to use in constructing the poem.

3. To find more themes, search for conceptual relationships between the categories you represented in your first poems (Glaser, 1978), a meta-coding of your poems. For example, I wrote more poems about the idea of mothering as an act of friendship (see "Mother/Daughter"). Thus, writing poems based on your initial coding poems may tell you even more about family. What I discovered in subsequent poems was that mother is a verb.

Exercise Four: The Group Poem/Exquisite Corpse

The group poem is a variation on poetic analysis and story telling that offers possibilities for connection to larger cultural issues. It can help us get unstuck from our usual habits of thought. It can help uncover group angst. This can be used in a class, a writing group, or even as a party game at a family gathering. I offer a variation of the game exquisite corpse, a kind of collaborative writing that may be of interest to you (e.g., http://www.poets.org/poetsorg/text/play-exquisite-corpse).

Background. Exquisite Corpse is a collaborative poetry game that was started by the Parisian Surrealists. It entails variations on collaborative artistic work with the goal of upturning usual habits of the mind to create something unique. The usual rule is that each person will not see what the other has written in order to allow for surprise and creative metaphors. I argue that playing a version of this game may help us restory, disclose, and re-member family secrets.

Family Secrets can be written about using *accidental ethnography* as a technique, what Chris Poulus (2008) suggested as a method to story our lives and bring forward what may be lost in our unconscious—eating disorders, stigmatized identities, suicide, abuse, and other difficult topics. This entails writing about dreams, clues, memories, and reflections from the unconscious, from seemingly "accidental signs and impulses that surge up and, from time to time, really grip us, take hold of us, call us out and throw us down, sweep us away, and carry us to places we may not have even imagined" (Poulus, 2008, p. 47). The goal of this kind of writing is to reveal and make conscious secrets that harm families and communities.

Accidental ethnography means writing and rewriting family secrets that haunt us and break into our day-to-day relating (anyway). "Telling the story, despite anxiety, is the path to healing. And, anyways, storytelling is far more potent, far more fascinating, far more engaging than secret-keeping" (Poulus, 2008, p. 187). If we write about hurtful secrets, if we reveal harmful patterns of interaction, then we may be able to tell better stories and offer more possibilities.

How To: Write answers to the following prompts.

- Describe something dangerous you did in the past.
- Describe something sinful or bad you did as a child.
- Describe an incident that filled you with dread.
- What is the most embarrassing thing that has ever happened to you?
- What is one of your earliest memories? What is the overriding emotion you attach to this memory?
- What is a moment where you remember feeling being unfairly treated?
- What are you most afraid of?
- What is one of your worst memories?
- What makes you angry?
- Have you told anyone in your family the answers to the questions above? Why or why not?
- What are some stories that your family tells (or does not tell) about members in the family? What are some stories they tell about those outside of the family (e.g., divorce, infidelity)?

Next, write down some details to one of the answers above. Choose and answer that you want to explore and that has emotional resonance with you. What impact did this have on your life?

Version One: Group Poem Construction

Decide on the form of the poem beforehand. You could have players write words in a pattern (e.g., noun, verb, adjective, noun). You could have players write lines of poetry (e.g., a vivid memory). Based on the writing prompts, choose the first line to a poem. When you finish writing a line, fold the paper over before passing it to the next person.

Some variations to this game: Choose to look at the preceding lines or not. Decide to not use a predetermined form.

Version Two: Three Poems and Responses

You could write three different poems: one about a childhood memory (e.g., "When the preacher came by the house after our year absence," in which I remember my father telling the Baptist preacher that we were no longer going to attend church because of his bigotry), a poem where the structure matches the experience you want to write about (e.g., "Cancer Sonnet"), or family secrets such as adultery (e.g., "In the Court of Common Pleas").

After you write a poem, share the poem and have another person write a poem in response to your poem. You could write a response to the poem and so on. This could generate a series of poems.

REFERENCES

Alcoff, L. M. (2003). Introduction. In L. M. Alcoff (Ed.), *Singing in the fire: Stories of women in philosophy* (pp. 1-13). Lanham, MD: Rowman & Littlefield.

Baxter, L. (2011). *Voicing relationships: A dialogic perspective.* Thousand Oaks, CA: Sage.

Baxter, L. A., & Braithwaite, D. O. (Eds.). (2008). *Engaging theories in interpersonal communication: Multiple perspectives.* Thousand Oaks, CA: Sage.

Beck, S. J., Miller, A. N., & Frahm, W. A. (2012). An alternative approach to family communication: Studying the family from a group communication perspective. In C. T. Salmon (Ed.), *Communication yearbook 35* (pp. 93-117). New York: Routledge.

Butler-Kisber, L. (2002). Artful portrayals in qualitative inquiry: The road to found poetry and beyond. *The Alberta Journal of Educational Research, XLVIII*(3), 229-239.

Calafell, B. M. (2004). Disrupting the dichotomy: 'Yo Soy Chicana/o?' in the new Latina/o South. *The Communication Review, 7,* 175-204.

Carr, J. M. (2003). Poetic expressions of vigilance. *Qualitative Health Research, 13,* 1324-1331.

Dailey, R. M. (2006). Confirmation in parent-adolescent relationships and adolescent openness: Toward extending confirmation theory. *Communication Monographs, 73,* 434-458.

Dailey, R. M. (2010). Testing components of confirmation: How acceptance and challenge from mothers, fathers, and siblings are related to adolescent self-concept. *Communication Monographs, 77*(4), 592–617.

Denzin, N. K. (2014). *Interpretive autoethnography* (2nd ed.). Thousand Oaks, CA: Sage.

Doty, M. (2010). *The art of description: World into word.* Minneapolis, MN: Graywolf Press.

Drury, J. (2006). *The poetry dictionary* (2nd ed.). Cincinnati, OH: Writer's Digest Books.

Ellis, C. (1995). *Final negotiations.* Philadelphia: Temple University Press.

Ellis, C. (2007). Telling secrets, revealing lives: Relational ethics in research with intimate others. *Qualitative Inquiry, 13*(1), 3-29.

Faulkner, S. L. (2009). *Poetry as method: Reporting research through verse.* Walnut Creek, CA: Left Coast Press.

Faulkner, S. L. (2012a). Frogging it: A poetic analysis of relationship dissolution. *Qualitative Research in Education, 1*(2), 202-227. doi: 10.4471.qre.2012.08

Faulkner, S. L. (2012b). That baby will cost you: An intended ambivalent pregnancy. *Qualitative Inquiry, 18*(4), 333-340.

Faulkner, S. L. (Ed.). (2013). *Inside relationships: A creative case book on relational communication.* Walnut Creek, CA: Left Coast Press.

Faulkner, S. L. (2014). Bad mom(my) litany: Spanking cultural myths of middle-class motherhood. *Cultural Studies <=> Critical Methodologies, 14(2),* 138-146. doi: 10.1177/1532708613512270

Faulkner, S. L., Calafell, B. M., & Grimes, D. S. (2009). Hello Kitty goes to college: Poems about harassment in the academy. In M. Prendergast, C. Leggo, & P. Sameshima (Eds.), *Poetic inquiry: Vibrant voices in the social sciences* (pp. 187-208). Rotterdam: Sense Publishers.

Faulkner, S. L., & Ruby, P. D. (in press). Feminist constructions of identity in romantic relationships: A relational dialectics analysis of email discourse through the use of collaborative found poetry. *Women's Studies in Communication.*

Faulkner, S. L. & Hecht, M. L. (2011). The negotiation of closetable identities: A narrative analysis of LGBTQ Jewish identity. *Journal of Social and Personal Relationships, 28*(6), 829-847. doi: 10.1177/0265407510391338

Furman, R. (2006). Poetry as research: Advancing scholarship and the development of poetry therapy as a profession. *The Journal of Poetry Therapy, 19*(3), 133-145.

Furman, R., Langer, C. L., Davis, C. S., Gallardo, H. P., & Kulkarni, S. (2007). Expressive, research and reflective poetry as qualitative inquiry: A study of adolescent identity. *Qualitative Research, 7*(3), 301-315.

REFERENCES

Furman, R., Lietz, C., & Langer, C. L. (2006). The research poem in international social work: Innovations in qualitative methodology. *International Journal of Qualitative Methods, 5*(3), Article 3. Retrieved June 24, 2014 from http://www.ualberta.ca/~iiqm/backissues/5_3/pdf/ furman.pdf

Galvin, K. M. (2006). Diversity's impact on defining the family: Discourse dependence and identity. In L. H. Turner & R. West (Eds.), *The family communication sourcebook* (pp. 3-20). Thousand Oaks, CA: Sage.

Galvin, K. M., Brummel, B. J., & Bylund, C. L. (2004). *Family communication: Cohesion and change* (6th ed). New York: Pearson.

Gingrich-Philbrook, C. (2005). Autoethnography's family values: Easy access to compulsory experiences. *Text and Performance Quarterly, 25*(4), 297-314.

Graham, D., & Sontag, K. Containing multitudes. In K. Sontag & D. Graham (Eds.), *After confession: Poetry as autobiography* (pp. 3-8). Saint Paul, MN: Graywolf Press

Hoagland, T. (2006). *Real sofistikashun: Essays on poetry and craft.* Saint Paul, MN: Graywolf Press.

Hugo, R. (1992). *The triggering town: Lectures and essays on poetry and writing.* New York: W. W. Norton & Company.

Glaser, B. G. (1978). *Theoretical sensitivity: Advances in the methodology of grounded theory.* Mill Valley, CA: Sociology Press.

Glesne, C. (1997). That rare feeling: re-presenting research through poetic transcription. *Qualitative Inquiry, 3,* 202-222.

Koerner, A. F., & Fitzpatrick, M. A. (2008). Family communication patterns theory: A social cognitive approach. In L. A. Baxter & D. O. Braithwaite (Eds.), *Engaging theories in interpersonal communication: Multiple perspectives* (pp. 50-65). Thousand Oaks, CA: Sage.

Lieblich, A., Tuval-Mashiach, R., & Zilber, T. (1998). *Narrative research: Reading, analysis, and interpretation.* Thousand Oaks, CA: Sage.

Lindlof, T. R., & Taylor, B. C. (2011). *Qualitative communication research methods* (3rd ed.). Thousand Oaks, CA: Sage.

Madison, D. S. (1991). "That was my occupation": Oral narrative, performance, and black feminist thought. *Text and Performance Quarterly, 13,* 213-232.

Madison, D. S. (2004). Performance, personal narratives, and the politics of possibility. In Y. S. Lincoln & N. K. Denzin (Eds.), *Turning points in qualitative research: Tying knots in a handkerchief* (pp. 469-486). Walnut Creek, CA: AltaMira.

McAdams, D. P. (1993). *The stories we live by: Personal myths and the making of the self.* New York: William Morrow.

Notely, A. (1998). *Mysteries of small houses.* New York: Penguin Books.

Owen, W. F. (1984). Interpretive themes in relational communication. *Quarterly Journal of Speech, 70,* 274-287.

Padgett, R. (Ed.) (1987). *The teachers and writers handbook of poetic forms.* New York: Teachers & Writers Collaborative.

Parini, J. (2008). *Why poetry matters.* New Haven, CT: Yale University Press.

Pelias, R. J. (2005). Performative writing as scholarship: An apology, an argument, an anecdote. *Cultural Studies ⇔ Critical Methodologies, 5*(4), 415-424.

Pelias, R. J. (2011). *Leaning: A poetics of personal relations.* Walnut Creek, CA: Left Coast Press.

Petronio, S. (2002). *Boundaries of privacy: Dialectics of disclosure.* Albany: State University of New York Press.

Pipher, M. (1997). *The shelter of each other: Rebuilding our families.* New York: Ballantine Books.

Poulus, C. N. (2008). *Accidental ethnography: An inquiry into family secrecy.* Walnut Creek, CA: Left Coast Press, Inc.

Prendergast, M. (2009). "*Poem* is what?": Poetic inquiry in qualitative social science research. In M. Prendergast, C. Leggo, & P. Sameshima (Eds.), *Poetic inquiry: Vibrant voices in the social sciences* (pp. xix-xli). Rotterdam: Sense Publishers.

Riessman, C. K. (1993). *Narrative analysis.* Newbury Park, CA: Sage.

Revell, D. (2007). *The art of attention: A poet's eye.* Minneapolis, MN: Graywolf Press.

Rose, D. (1990). *Living the ethnographic life*. Thousand Oaks, CA: Sage.

Richardson, L. (2002). Poetic representations of interviews. In J. F. Gubrium & J. A. Holstein (Eds.), *Handbook of interview research: Context and method* (pp. 877-891). Thousand Oaks, CA: Sage.

Simic, C. (1990). *Wonderful words, silent truth: Essays on poetry and a memoir*. Ann Arbor, MI: The University of Michigan Press.

Stoller, D. (2003). *Stich 'n bitch: The knitter's handbook*. New York: Workman Publishing Company

Stone, E. (2003). Family ground rules. In K. M. Galvin & P. J Cooper (Eds.), *Making connections: Readings in relational communication* (3rd ed., pp. 70-78). Los Angeles, CA: Roxbury Publishing.

Todres, L. & Galvin, K. T. (2008). Embodied interpretation: A novel way of evocatively re-presenting meanings in phenomenological research. *Qualitative Research, 8(5)*, 568-583. doi: 10.1177/1468794108094866

Young, D. (2010). *The art of recklessness: Poetry as assertive force and contradiction*. Minneapolis, MN: Graywolf Press.

Walker, F. X. (2008). *When winter come: The ascension of York*. Lexington, KY: University Press of Kentucky.

Walker, F. X. (2013). *Turn me loose: The unghosting of Medgar Evers*. Athens, GA: The University of Georgia Press.

Walsh, S. (2006). An Irigarayan framework and resymbolization in an arts-informed research process. *Qualitative Inquiry, 12*(5), 976-993.

Wilmot, W. (2003). The relational perspective. In K. M. Galvin & P. J. Cooper (Eds.), *Making connections: Readings in relational communication* (3rd ed., pp. 11-19). Los Angeles: Roxbury.

Wood, J. T. (2002). What's a family, anyway? Different views of what family means. In J. Stewart (Ed.), *Bridges not walls: A book about interpersonal communication* (8th ed., pp. 289-298). New York: McGraw Hill.

Young, D. (2010). *The art of recklessness: Poetry as assertive force and contradiction*. Minneapolis, MN: Graywolf Press.